TIME

100 American Originals

The Things That Shaped Our Culture

The Indian Scout motorcycle. Since 1920.

CONTENTS

O BRAVE NEW WORLD Televisions get a final inspection as they pass through the RCA Victor plant in Camden, N.J., July 1950.

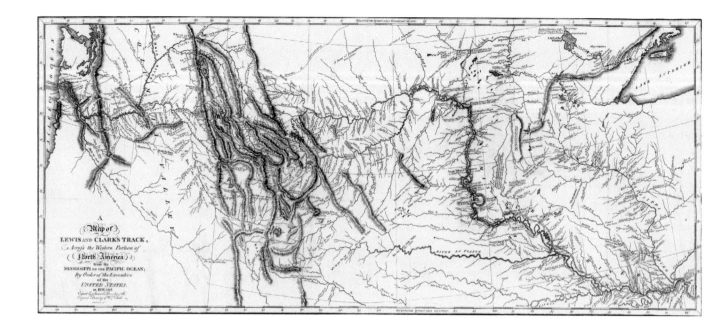

A Map of LEWIS AND CLARKS TRACK, Across the Western Portion of North America from the MISSISSIPI to the PACIFIC OCEAN; By Order of the Executive of the UNITED STATES.

INTRODUCTION

What Defines America?

By Daniel S. Levy

AMERICA IS MANY THINGS. A LAND. A CONCEPT. A home. Ever since our nation's founding in Philadelphia in 1776, people have sought to define the United States. But America is unique—hard to categorize or describe. One way to try is through some of the seminal entities, items and ideas that were born or nurtured on this soil. These are what this special edition of TIME calls "American originals."

For the past 240 years (or longer, really), Americans have been building, tinkering, inventing, singing, dancing, writing, playing, working, imagining and reimagining themselves and this country, all within the context of a notion: the American dream. This is a country of seekers and creators eager to see and influence what

THIS LAND IS OUR LAND In 1814, cartographers published a map [above] that delineated the territory Lewis and Clark crossed during their epic two-year hike to the Pacific. On the facing page, a few of the choices we agonized over as we searched for the ultimate American originals: Corvette [top] or Mustang? *The Wizard of Oz* or *Gone with the Wind*? Polaroid or Kodak Brownie?

lies ahead. Yet attempting to gather all that is original about America would be like trying to canvass every step of the land that the explorers Meriwether Lewis and William Clark and the members of their Corps of Discovery trekked across in the early 19th century: too vast, too overwhelming.

We restricted ourselves to 100 originals. It wasn't easy. Discussions of what to include on the list invariably led to passionate debate: Which movie, *The Wizard of Oz* or *Gone with the Wind*? Which camera, Kodak or Polaroid? To make our decisions, we thought first about what is essential and what has changed society. Take the Mustang and the Corvette. Both are iconic American cars, but the Mustang altered the driving habits of a nation while setting off an age in which cars that were designed to be fun (and not simply utilitarian) were affordable for many. Quandaries abounded. There's nothing more American than mom, apple pie and baseball, of course. But, well, we had to concede that "mom" is not exactly a uniquely American concept. As for apple pie? That was probably first baked in medieval England. Baseball, of course, needed to be included—it's our "national pastime," after all—and it can be found, with a particular twist, in the Leisure chapter on page 88.

Some choices were unassailable: the Declaration of Independence, because it merged 13 disparate colonies into America; the Wright brothers' plane, because it allowed humankind to so powerfully slip the grip of gravity; the teddy bear, since we all need a nonjudgmental best buddy. In the end, we hope we have amassed a list that is not only original but also includes things that have had a profound influence on the country and, often, the world. We hope that within these pages you will learn some new things about your favorite American originals, as well as come across a few others that will join your personal best list.

ICONIC OBJECTS

1. The Declaration of Independence

IT IS A WISP OF PARCHMENT MEASURING a mere 24½ by 29¾ inches. Yet the vision, the clarity and the gravitas in its faded words transcend the document's frailties. The Declaration of Independence laid out the American colonists' grievances and, more important, proclaimed their sacred rights and their fervent dream. It was a daring call for rebellion by a disparate group telling its mother country, the most powerful nation on earth, of its determination to be free. The job of drafting this history-altering document—of giving form to aspiration, eloquence to desire—was entrusted to Thomas Jefferson. The 33-year-old Virginian had spent his life immersed in the works of philosophers such as John Locke and David Hume, and over a few days during the hot Philadelphia summer of 1776, Jefferson distilled the best of the Enlightenment and put down his democratic thoughts. Although he said he was not trying for any sort of "originality of principle or sentiment," Jefferson succinctly codified what he called the "expression of the American mind," summarizing near the start a creed for a hopeful nation: "We hold these truths to be self-evident, that all men are created equal." This proclamation was a just necessity, as were such basic rights as "Life, Liberty and the pursuit of Happiness." What Jefferson wrote, and what the delegates later ratified, was treasonous; Benjamin Franklin underscored their precarious state by noting, "We must all hang together, or assuredly we shall all hang separately." Yet for more than two centuries, the message of Jefferson's words has endured and spread. It has touched all in America and been a basis for enlightened thought far and wide: in France, with the 1789 Declaration of the Rights of Man and of the Citizen; at the 1848 Seneca Falls Convention in New York, where female suffragists issued a Declaration of Sentiments; in early stages of Martin Luther King Jr.'s 1963 "I Have a Dream" speech. The assertion of independence is so large an idea that it needs no adornment, which may be why the back of the document says, simply, "Original Declaration of Independence, dated 4th July 1776."

2. The Liberty Bell

LIKE SO MANY OTHERS IN THIS nation, this 2,080-pound symbol of American freedom is an immigrant. Created in London in 1751 to commemorate the 50th anniversary of the signing of William Penn's Charter of Privileges, the bell first cracked when it was tried out in Philadelphia. It was soon recast, and, with a verse from the Bible's book of Leviticus encircling the top, the bell announced its purpose to "Proclaim liberty throughout all the land unto all the inhabitants thereof." The Pennsylvania State House used it to alert lawmakers and the public of meetings. It has been claimed that it chimed the news of the Continental Congress's adoption of the Declaration of Independence. In its key of E-flat, the bell continued to ring out calls for freedom, but it developed another crack sometime in the 1840s. "The old Independence Bell rang its last clear note on Monday last in honor of the birthday of [George] Washington," reported the *Philadelphia Public Ledger* on Feb. 26, 1846, "and now hangs in the great city steeple irreparably cracked and dumb." Yet even in silence, the Liberty Bell continued to resound with power. Abolitionists adopted it as a symbol in the fight against slavery, and by the end of the 19th century, most Americans identified the bell as a representation of freedom and a reminder of the country's early days. Throughout the 20th century, its message reverberated in the fights for women's suffrage and civil rights, and now more than a million visitors each year see the bell, taking that message into the years ahead.

3. The American Flag

THOUGH THE STARS AND STRIPES HAS evolved over its long life, it has a lasting and enduring look, an iconic sensibility. Traditional belief holds that Philadelphia seamstress Betsy Ross made it, but it was most probably created by Declaration of Independence signer Francis Hopkinson. Charles Thomson, who served as secretary at the Continental Congress and wrote out the Declaration, summed up the flag's symbolism when he noted that white stood for "purity and innocence," red for "hardiness & valour" and blue for "vigilence, perseverence [sic] & justice." The Continental Congress formally approved the tricolor banner with its 13 stripes and its circle of 13 stars in June 1777.

That flag changed as America grew, adding stars and stripes with the admission of new states. It was a 15-star and 15-stripe flag that Francis Scott Key watched survive "the rockets' red glare, the bombs bursting in air" during the British attack on Fort McHenry in the War of 1812. In 1818, Congress mandated that although a star would be added for each new state, the stripes would forever refer to the original 13. With 50 stars ever since Hawaii joined the union in 1959, Old Glory is a tangible, malleable symbol. Children pledge their allegiance to the flag at the start of school days; families unfurl it on national holidays; fans turn to the flag, caps over hearts, at the beginning of ballgames; citizens wrap themselves in its colors to proclaim their rights or to protest the lack of them; soldiers wear the flag on their sleeves, literally; and we sometimes have to drape the coffins of our fallen heroes with that flag, when they have made the ultimate sacrifice for the nation it represents.

4. The United States Constitution

WHILE FREE AND INDEPENDENT, the United States was, in its early years, far from united. When peace arrived in 1783, the nation's initial constitution, the Articles of Confederation, merely cobbled together a loose alliance of states. And though the articles gave the central government certain powers, Congress lacked the ability to call up troops or obtain needed monies. To reframe the ineffective system, representatives of the 13 states headed back to Philadelphia in 1787 to form a more perfect union, splicing into the DNA of America the ability to grow and evolve. That Constitution, which was ratified on June 21, 1788, laid out the rules by which the American government would operate, setting its composition, power and limitations within a tripartite construction of checks and balances. What the representatives fashioned is a living, breathing system open to change. And change came quickly, in December 1791, with the inclusion of the first 10 amendments. Known as the Bill of Rights, it protects such practices as religion, free speech and the bearing of arms. Since then, the Constitution has been amended 17 more times, ending slavery, allowing for an income tax, giving women the right to vote and abolishing poll taxes. Just as the Declaration of Independence has inspired people around the world to seek democratic freedom, the Constitution has served as a model for other nations in building effective governments that ensure the rights of their citizens.

5. Campaign Memorabilia

EVERY FOUR YEARS, AMERICANS HEAD to the polls to decide on the next president, and on a smaller scale they vote each fall to select their congressional representatives, mayors, council members and sheriffs. Nothing crystallizes and manipulates the choosing of our candidates like classic campaign buttons—a marriage of seriousness and sloganeering; a mix of hope, humor and hype. Buttons (and posters of a similar spirit) are as old as the presidency. When George Washington took the oath of office in April 1789, his close supporters sewed copper buttons to their lapels bearing his initials, GW, encircled by such phrases as LONG LIVE THE PRESIDENT and UNITY, PROSPERITY & INDEPENDENCE. Images started making their way onto buttons with Abraham Lincoln's run in 1860. The pin-backed campaign button that we know today arrived in 1896 during

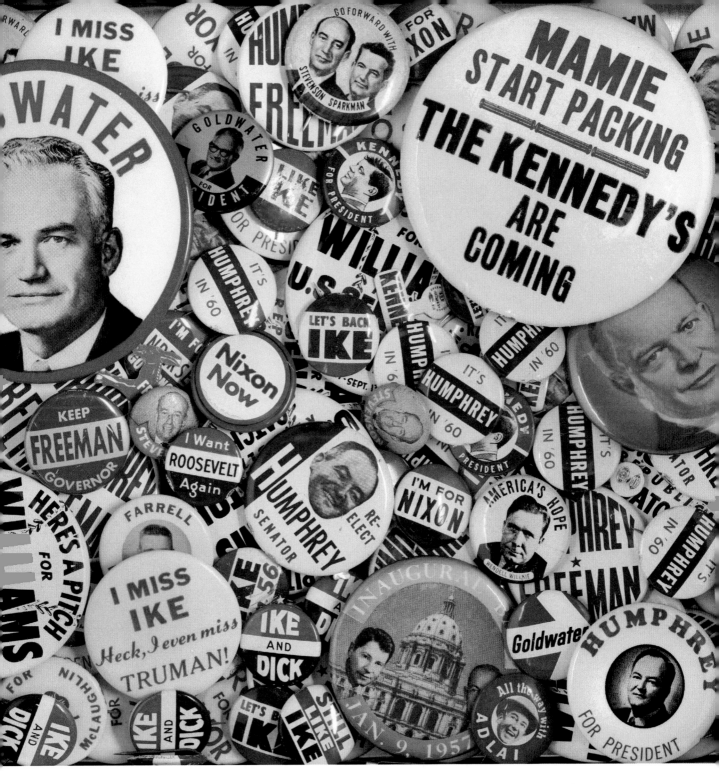

the race between William Jennings Bryan and William McKinley. It was made possible by the creation of celluloid, which allowed a thin, protective coating to cover the images. Posters plastered on walls and nailed to outdoor fences offered more space (as, over time, did bumper stickers), as well as text that tended to be far from subtle. Bold graphics either sold a dream or warned of a nightmare. John Quincy Adams talked of Andrew Jackson's "bloody deeds."

James Garfield extolled his background as an industrious farmer. Opponents of Dwight D. Eisenhower warned of electing a "career officer." And Barack Obama became the embodiment of HOPE. Many of the Democratic and Republican candidates who went unelected—not to mention those from the Federalist, Whig, Know Nothing, Progressive and States' Rights Democratic parties of yesteryear—have receded from memory, but their memorabilia imprints survive.

6–7. The Blue and Gray Uniforms of the Civil War

THE BLUE AND GRAY UNIFORMS WERE as different as the Northern (blue) and Southern (gray) men who wore them. Blue had been a regulation color of U.S. Army uniforms since the Revolutionary War. It is believed that "cadet gray" was adopted by the Confederates because it was the standard color of the American state militia uniform. And so, to combat Billy Yank—wearing his blue flannel coat and trousers and blue forage cap—Johnny Reb put on his gray wool jacket and pants. Ultimately the color didn't matter: after four ghastly years of battle and the deaths of more than 600,000 soldiers, both uniforms were drenched in red American blood. Although Confederate commander

8–13. **America's Hats**

TRICORNE HAT

COONSKIN CAP

COWBOY HAT

DOUGHBOY HAT

CONSTRUCTION HAT

BASEBALL CAP

HATS DO MORE THAN SHIELD FROM RAIN AND the sun. A hat might represent rank and status, flaunt an attitude, make a fashion statement or declare love for a sports team. Certain hats represent the breadth and range of American history. Although the black felt tricornered hat—or tricorne—might have originated in Europe, the sight of its three sides folded up to create a wedge around one's head "like a mince pie" vividly brings to mind the 18th-century revolutionaries who liberated the land from England. The coonskin cap made from raccoon pelts—a head covering adapted from Native American caps—evokes the sense of American exploration and exceptionalism, of the lone frontiersman (Davy Crockett, say) trudging through a snow-blanketed terrain. Once manifest destiny played out across the continent, the land needed to be tamed; a variation on the broad-brimmed Mexican sombrero was called for. For all those cowboys, John Stetson in 1865 created the waterproof and durable Boss of the Plains hat. With its pinched crown and curved brim, it was a much-needed accessory, well suited to the rugged trails. As soldiers headed to World War I, the doughboys doffed their broad-brimmed campaign hats. They served as a symbol of the U.S.'s arrival as a world power and opened the first act of the American Century. Soon skyscrapers soared, dams regulated rivers, highways spread and housing developments sprouted. These were erected by construction workers in their hard hats, which represented American engineering might and the emergence of a growing middle class. And with the financial security of the postwar years came time for leisure: barbecues, road trips and, of course, the American pastime, embodied by the baseball caps scrunched over countless heads on sandlots just as on major-league fields.

in chief Robert E. Lee surrendered at Appomattox Court House on April 9, 1865, and General Ulysses S. Grant wrote that "The war is over, the Rebels are our countrymen again," Americans of all persuasions have developed an obsession with this fratricidal war. Such works as *The Birth of a Nation, Gone with the Wind, Cold Mountain* and *Gods and Generals* have explored the hopes, dreams and fears of all who donned those uniforms. For more than six decades, ending in 2003, a college football all-star game pitting players from old Confederate states against those from old Union states took place in Alabama, typically on Christmas Day. And each year, to this day, tens of thousands of men, women and children slip on their garb, unfurl their Stars and Stripes or Stars and Bars, set up camps and line up along battlefields to re-enact the war's events, partly as a way to understand the causes that compelled their ancestors—brothers, fathers, cousins, uncles, friends and neighbors—to make that fateful choice to wear either the blue or the gray.

14. The Golden Spike

DURING THE EARLY TO MID-1800S, much of America's land was on its way to being settled. But getting from sea to shining sea—that is, from the Atlantic coast to the Pacific—proved arduous. Travelers had three unpalatable options: the dangerous 3,000-mile wagon ride across the plains, the perilous 14,000-mile route around South America, or the deadly trip down to Panama, over the Isthmus of Panama and back up the West Coast. With the discovery of gold in California in the late 1840s, a wave of migration began, with more than 300,000 people heading west by the early 1850s. Americans needed a better way to get there. Work on a transcontinental railroad began in 1863, with the Union Pacific laying tracks westward from Omaha, Neb., while the Central Pacific set off eastward from Sacramento, Calif.

Workers needed six and a half years to cut paths in forests, ford rivers, blast through mountains and lay the lines. The two sides met up near the Great Salt Lake at Promontory, Utah, on May 10, 1869. There they laid the last few feet of the Transcontinental Railroad. As California governor Leland Stanford and Union Pacific president Thomas Durant took turns driving down a nearly one-pound ceremonial golden spike inscribed "May God continue the unity of our country as this railroad unites the two great oceans of the world," celebrants raised toasts and telegraphs shot the news in both directions. Coast-to-coast travel time went from half a year to less than a week, a development that revolutionized America. Western goods could be shipped quickly east, immigrants could head west much more easily, and the nation's interior was further established.

15–16. **Uncle Sam and Rosie the Riveter**

MAYBE THEY'RE RELATED. HE IS an elderly gentleman with a star-encircled hat, a blue frock coat, a red tie and long white hair who looks like a cross between your mother's favorite brother and a circus performer. She is the proto–career woman, with power tools and a can-do attitude; you could see her as his niece. Together, Uncle Sam and Rosie the Riveter urged American families to defend their land; their lineage is nearly as old as the nation. Uncle Sam, who melds Yankee Doodle and the rural wit Brother Jonathan, may have first taken form during the War of 1812. Back then, Troy, N.Y., businessman Samuel Wilson supplied the Army with barrels of beef stamped "U.S.," and the mark evolved into the nickname Uncle Sam. At first, cartoonists drew him as a thin man with whiskers and a tall hat, but the uncle we know today is a creation of the pen and brush of James Montgomery Flagg. His determined, hat-topped Uncle Sam implored young men during World War I to sign up, telling them "I Want You." And they quickly answered their uncle's call, with America mustering a force of 4 million doughboys. When the next world war arrived, the government turned its attention to women; with 16 million men in the military, there was a shortage of workers on the home front. Hoping to recruit women for the munitions industry, the Westinghouse Electric and Manufacturing Company had artist J. Howard Miller create a poster of a working woman flexing her muscles and declaring, "We Can Do It!" The image of Rosie the Riveter was then perfected by Norman Rockwell in May 1943 for the *Saturday Evening Post*. In Rockwell's vision, Rosie is a brawny, rivet-gun-wielding Amazon stepping on a copy of Adolf Hitler's *Mein Kampf*—clearly a gal the Axis powers shouldn't mess with. The campaign worked. That year, women made up 65% of aviation-industry workers, and by 1945 nearly a quarter of married women worked. There was even a popular song called "Rosie the Riveter," with the lyrics "She's making history / Working for victory / Rosie the Riveter." And make history she did.

17. The Hollywood Sign

HOLLYWOOD IS A TOWN OF OVER-sized dreams and shining stars—a place, Marilyn Monroe said, "where they'll pay you a thousand dollars for a kiss and 50 cents for your soul." With its warm weather and vivid sunshine, the area attracted filmmakers in the nascent years of cinema, with one of the first films, *The Count of Monte Cristo*, being shot there in 1908. Soon producers such as Cecil B. DeMille, D.W. Griffith and Samuel Goldwyn set up shop, and Los Angeles became the center of the film industry. The city loves to fete itself—see the handprints of movie stars encased in cement at the TCL Chinese Theatre on Hollywood Boulevard or the Walk of Fame that runs down that street and along Vine. But nothing greets the starry-eyed visitors more conspicuously than the 350-foot-long string of letters perched on a hill overlooking the City of Dreams. The HOLLYWOOD sign, created in 1923 by *Los Angeles Times* publisher Harry Chandler as a promotion for his upscale Hollywoodland real estate development, was born ready for its close-up. It debuted in the 1936 film *Hollywood Boulevard* and has graced the big screen many times in the decades since. (Its appearance in 2011's *Friends with Benefits* stands out.) Constructed from metal squares and lit to blink in succession—"Holly," "Wood," "Land"—the 43-foot-high sign was intended to last for a year or two. Like some lucky stars, it survived, even as its youthful glow dimmed and it neared middle age. In 1949 the Hollywood Chamber of Commerce gave it a needed face-lift, lipoing off the last four letters. And in the '70s, funds raised by local resident Hugh Hefner helped refurbish the sign once again so that it could continue to welcome new generations of movie stars and fans.

18. Smokey Bear

IN THE SPRING OF 1942, JUST AFTER AMERICA entered World War II, a Japanese submarine shelled an oil field close to Los Padres National Forest in California. The flames were extinguished, but with firefighters off at war, fear spread of the potential danger of vast conflagrations along the coast. The U.S. Forest Service organized the Cooperative Forest Fire Prevention Program and, with the help of the War Advertising Council, launched a campaign with posters that warned, "Forest Fires Aid the Enemy." Disney had just released *Bambi*, and the movie studio allowed the forest service to enlist the title creature in the campaign—but only briefly. So in 1944 the service had illustrator Albert Stahle create a new character. Stahle's artwork showed a bear wearing a ranger's hat as he hefted a shovel, doused a campfire and advised, "Care will prevent 9 out of 10 forest fires!" In a nation accustomed to the

warmth of teddy bears—which, incidentally, were named for the nature-loving president Theodore Roosevelt—Smokey Bear became vastly popular. Then, in the spring of 1950, a major fire swept through New Mexico's Capitan Mountains. As firefighters fought the flames, they found a lone cub. News services picked up the story, and, sensing the bear's potential as a fire-safety ambassador, the forest service named him Smokey Bear and found him a home at Washington's National Zoo, where he was a favorite attraction. Smokey Bear's image has since appeared on countless posters and prevention campaigns and proved highly effective as America's longest-running public-service campaign. The furry pitch guy's good work is still needed. From 2010 to 2014, the federal government spent some $8 billion fighting fires, with more than 30 million acres of land affected by 325,000 separate blazes.

19. Santiago Calatrava's Train Station

THIS WAS THE SPOT WHERE, ON THE morning of Sept. 11, 2001, radical fundamentalists flew airplanes into the World Trade Center's twin towers. As rescue workers frantically scoured the site, photographer Thomas Franklin captured three New York firefighters raising the Stars and Stripes. The image evoked Joe Rosenthal's Pulitzer Prize–winning shot of Marines hoisting the U.S. flag on the Pacific island of Iwo Jima on Feb. 23, 1945, and it reminded Americans how they had triumphed in the past over adversity and that the United States would still not be cowed. The deaths in New York of 3,000 Americans made this a 16-acre wound in the heart of the land. But slowly that section of lower Manhattan

healed: a new lofty tower was built, new streets were laid out, and a memorial and museum were opened to honor those lost. Nothing, though, symbolizes the soaring spirit of the city and the nation more than Santiago Calatrava's World Trade Center Transportation Hub. The curved white building, dubbed the Oculus, suggests a winged phoenix rising from the ashes, bringing with it a new era of creativity and purpose. It is beautiful and inspirational—and highly functional. Calatrava's center, which opened on March 3, 2016, links nearly a dozen subway lines and underground pedestrian connections, as well as trains and ferries to New Jersey, tightly stitching the downtown area back into the fabric of the city and the nation.

Daniel Chester French and the Lincoln Memorial Statue

THE LINCOLN MEMORIAL is a civic temple to a fallen hero of democracy, a president who preserved the union and was assassinated just days after the end of the Civil War. Looming at the western end of the National Mall along the Potomac River, the classical building was designed by Illinois-born architect Henry Bacon and dedicated in May 1922. More than 50,000 people attended the opening, including then-president Warren G. Harding, former president and Supreme Court chief justice William Howard Taft and Robert Todd Lincoln, Abraham's sole surviving son, who had been present at his death in Washington 57 years earlier. As in ancient temples, a statue of a luminous figure commands the sanctuary. Here, gazing on the reflecting pool, sits Daniel Chester French's monumental figure of Lincoln. French, who was 10 when the Civil War began, started work on the commission in 1915. Working out of his home studio in Stockbridge, Mass., the sculptor prepared models of various ideas, basing his figure of the president on photos by Civil War photographer Mathew Brady as well as on casts of Lincoln's hands and face. The resulting 19-foot statue is made of 28 blocks of gleaming Georgia marble and took more than a year to carve. "What I wanted to convey," French said, "was the mental and physical strength of the great war president and his confidence in his ability to carry the thing through to a successful finish." French presented the 16th president as a kind father, pensive judge, strong leader and Great Emancipator. He sits in the heart of the memorial, bathed in an ethereal light. On the wall around him are carved inscriptions of soaring words from his Gettysburg and second inaugural addresses. And although the dedication was—perhaps ironically—segregated, the memorial has since welcomed all, especially those seeking the rights that Lincoln represented. It was here that Martin Luther King Jr. delivered his "I Have a Dream" speech in 1963 on the 100th anniversary of Lincoln's freeing of the slaves.

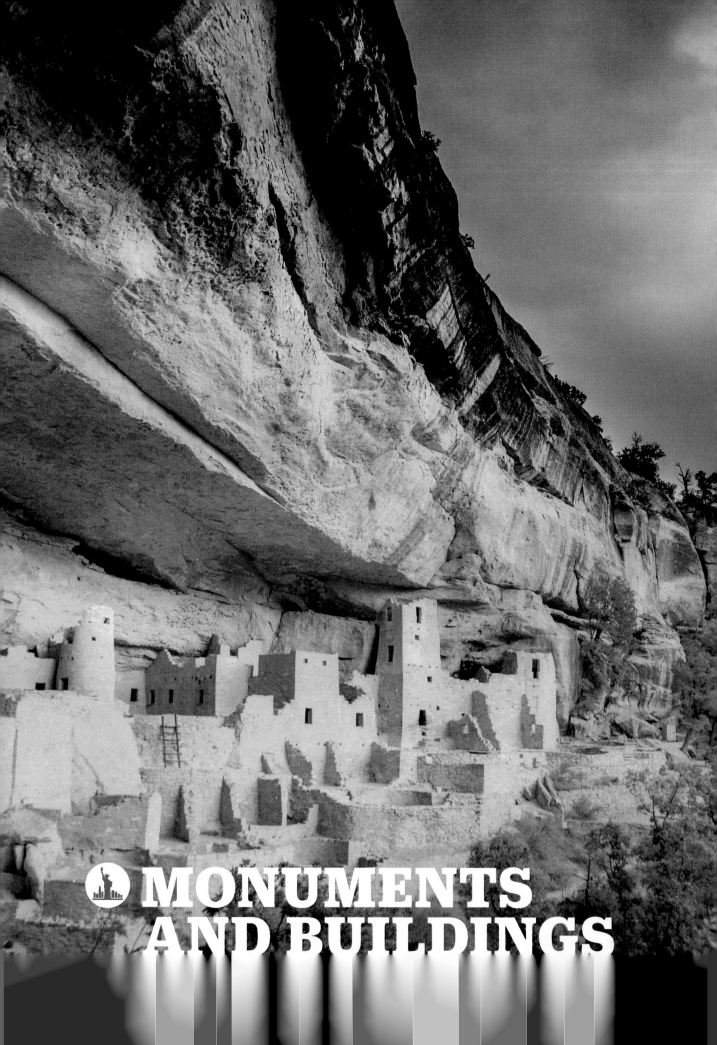

MONUMENTS AND BUILDINGS

20–24. Native American Buildings: Cahokia, Tepee, Wickiup, Cliff Palace and Pueblo

THE STRUCTURES ARE THE SEMINAL buildings of America, and their breadth of styles speaks to the richness of Native American life. More than 600 tribes once stretched across what is now the United States. Although many Americans think of Native American homes as simple tepees, the range of forms created were as varied as the tribes and were perfectly suited to their environments and lifestyles. Some of the structures were large, such as the 100-foot-tall Monks Mound at Cahokia, a six-square-mile site near present-day St. Louis. Cahokia flourished from 950 to 1350 and was the largest urban development north of Mexico. It boasted 120 massive earthwork mounds, huge plazas for ceremonies and games, and some 20,000 urban dwellers who belonged to the Middle Mississippian culture. The small and portable tepee served the nomadic Plains people. Often made of buffalo skins stretched across a cone-shaped framework of poles and decorated with paintings representing the hunt, these homes proved ideal for a life on the move in search of traveling herds. Algonquins in the Northeast lived in wickiups (wigwams), houses that could stretch some 20 feet in length and were fashioned from bent saplings to create a domelike structure, then sheathed with bark and mats. In the arid Southwest, the ancestral Anasazi created cliff-hugging dwellings from stone and adobe that often could be reached only by a ladder, which could be pulled up in case of an attack. Some, such as the fortress-like Cliff Palace in Mesa Verde National Park, contained hundreds of rooms. There are now low-to-the-ground adobe pueblo buildings derived from the cliff structures. Built of sunbaked clay, sand and silt, these well-insulated homes can contain many units and extended families.

25. **Monticello**

IN THE 1730S, PETER JEFFERSON STARTED a tobacco plantation in the Piedmont region of Virginia. His son Thomas especially loved going with his father to a spot at the top of an 867-foot mountain, where they got to look at their land. After Peter died in 1757, the future president inherited 5,000 acres, and as a student of the ancients and the Renaissance, he sought to bring the glories of Europe to his home. In 1768, four years before marrying Martha Wayles Skelton, he started work on his dream house overlooking Charlottesville. This was no rush job. For four decades, Jefferson obsessively tinkered with the design for the aerie he called Monticello, Italian for "little mountain."

Channeling the work of Andrea di Pietro della Gondola, the 16th-century Italian architect nicknamed Palladio, Jefferson finally arrived in 1809 at a home that paid homage to the designer. The 35-room, redbrick and white-wood structure, with its imperial pedimented portico and soaring octagonal dome (as seen on the tails side of the nickel) is based on Palladio's Villa la Rotonda near Vicenza, Italy. With its innovative interior filled with such Jeffersonian designs as the double opening door and the spherical sundial, plus his collection of art, artifacts and archaeological objects, it was Jefferson's command center. From there he ran his estate, read books and mused on the future of the nation he helped create.

26. **The Capitol**

THE CAPITOL RISES AT THE TOP OF THE National Mall and faces the Washington Memorial. It was initially designed by the Caribbean-born William Thornton, and construction began in September 1793, with the Senate chamber opening in 1800 and the House wing in 1807. Thomas Jefferson proclaimed it "simple, noble, beautiful, excellently distributed and moderate in size." During the War of 1812, the British torched the Capitol along with the White House, but a driving rain saved both from complete destruction. Boston architect Charles Bulfinch finished the restoration of the buildings and linked the House and Senate areas, making it a place that French political commentator Alexis de Tocqueville called "a magnificent palace." Bulfinch also designed a domed central building, and as the nation grew, the building grew. In the 1850s, Philadelphia architect Thomas Ustick Walter fashioned a new cast-iron dome, basing his plan on Michelangelo's soaring cap of Saint Peter's Basilica in Rome. With the help of engineer Montgomery C. Meigs, he created a massive top made up of nearly 9 million pounds of cast-iron girders, plates, columns and ornaments. During the Civil War, Abraham Lincoln insisted that construction continue as a sign of the vibrancy of the Union he sought to

preserve. And in December 1863, three weeks after Lincoln delivered the Gettysburg Address, construction of the dome was sufficiently along to permit the installation atop it of Thomas Crawford's bronze Statue of Freedom. When the classically designed woman with flowing hair and a warrior's helmet was raised into place, a salute was given and answered by the 35 guns in the 12 forts around Washington. It was below that symbol of freedom that Lincoln's body would be laid in state, in the building's Rotunda.

27. The One-Room Schoolhouse

HERE WAS A PLACE FOR ALL TO LEARN. The offspring of farmers, laborers and immigrants walked long distances or rode horses to get to school and, once in their seats, fell under the watchful eyes of a lone teacher. Around the potbellied stoves and alongside the fireplaces in these clapboard or brick structures, lessons were taught, the larger world was discussed, and hopes for the future were dreamed. Tiny schools became centers for small towns, and at one time nearly all Americans had passed some of their days in them. John Adams taught at one in Worcester, Mass. Abraham Lincoln learned his lessons in a crude log cabin on Old Cumberland Road in Kentucky. Laura Ingalls

Wilder, who wrote the *Little House on the Prairie* books, recalled how as her family moved, she attended school in numerous such buildings, saying, "I went to 'little red schoolhouses' all over the West." She taught at one, too, and in her books, the mother and one of the daughters taught at them.

The concept of separating children by grades began in Massachusetts in 1848 and spread steadily throughout the country, yet as late as 1913, half of all American children still attended one-room schoolhouses; there were 190,000 of them standing in 1919. But as people migrated to cities, smaller schools consolidated into larger systems, and one-room schoolhouses closed. Today, there are a mere 200 left, relics of a slower and perhaps simpler age.

28. The Statue of Liberty

SHE GREETS ALL, HER RIGHT arm raising a torch that lights the entrance to New York Harbor. The Statue of Liberty has patiently done just that since October 1886, when President Grover Cleveland unveiled this gift from the people of France to America. The statue celebrated democracy, the end of the Civil War and the abolition of slavery. At 151 feet tall, Liberty is imposing, to say the least. But she is also warm, benevolent, welcoming and motherly, which is not surprising considering that sculptor Frédéric-Auguste Bartholi reportedly modeled her serene face on that of his own mother, Charlotte. Lady Liberty's other hand cradles a tablet bearing the date of American independence, along with a sonnet by Emma Lazarus intoning, "Give me your tired, your poor / Your huddled masses yearning to breathe free." And as a subtle and often unseen symbol of the freedom Liberty promises, at her feet lie the broken shackles of the Old World and of slavery. On a steel framework made by Gustave Eiffel (the designer of the Eiffel Tower) and a base by American architect Richard Morris Hunt, she is, like the light from her torch, a beacon for the millions who have arrived at and continue to stream past Liberty Island on their way to a new life.

29. The White Picket Fence

IN HIS 1914 POEM "MENDING WALL," Robert Frost noted that "good fences make good neighbors." Unlike brick and stone walls or the more off-putting barbed wire, the white picket fence politely defines property in a neighborly fashion. It declares the limits of one's private grounds and gives a sign that the American dream has been obtained, a family started. It was just such a border that Aunt Polly hoped her wayward nephew Tom Sawyer would paint with the "bucket of whitewash and a long-handled brush" in order to teach him responsibility. For as Aunt Polly knew, civility and hard work had to be instilled. And while Tom learned another lesson—that of persuading others to do what needed to be done—he got his crew to spiff up his aunt's yard and make the place look grand. The meaning of the fence has been glorified throughout our popular culture, from the neat little one circling the Cleaver family's home on Mapleton Drive in *Leave It to Beaver* to the fencing imagined around the "little pink houses" that John Mellencamp sings are "for you and me."

30. **The Chrysler Building**

THOUGH THE DEVELOPMENT IN THE LATE 19TH CENTURY OF steel structures made the construction of skyscrapers a possibility, it wasn't until the years between the world wars that an explosive arrival of new towers graced skylines from Chicago to Buenos Aires, New York to Shanghai. Seemingly freed from the orderly language of classicism, architects explored new styles and forms. Some truly mega-tall buildings, such as the Empire State Building, shot up. But it was William Van Alen's creation, the Chrysler Building—which, at 1,046 feet, was briefly the world's tallest structure—that blindingly outshone all others. That tower, built for the auto manufacturer Walter Chrysler, is an Art Deco love letter to the car. It drips with forceful grace, complete with touches that make reference to the firm's autos, such as a stainless-steel sunburst grill crown, gargantuan gargoyle eagle hood ornaments and disks that resemble hubcaps. The plush interior is set off by a three-story lobby awash in geometric red Moroccan marble, exotic-wood veneers and a sienna-colored floor. Especially today, the Chrysler Building is a beloved sight among the jumble of towers cramming the New York skyline.

31. **Movie Palaces**

THEY WERE PALACES FOR THE PEOPLE, grand architectural piles where for a dime, John and Jane Q. Public could find a seat in imperial splendor, watch their favorite stars flicker on the silver screen and catch up on the latest events through newsreels. By 1916, there were 21,000 movie houses in the U.S. But with increased numbers came a desire to top the competition, and architects outdid one another, designing, in effect, temples for the worship of cinema. To do this, they slathered on gilded decorations, strung up crystal chandeliers, laid intricate plush carpeting, and plastered and painted ceilings that sparkled like the night sky. Cities began to fill up with grand, gaudy, otherworldly hodgepodges; one in Manhattan was described as "Byzantine-Romanesque-Indo-Hindu-Sino-Moorish-Persian-Eclectic-Rococo-Deco." Some of these halls seated thousands, and for patrons during the jazz age and then the Great Depression, they offered an escape to another world, complete with body-shaking music from a Mighty Wurlitzer organ and crisply dressed ushers and matrons. Some even sported their own restaurants, art galleries and billiard rooms.

The antitrust case *United States v. Paramount Pictures Inc.* in the late 1940s forced large studios to divest their theaters, and with the rise of TV and the flight to the suburbs, as well as the high cost of theater maintenance, these urban palaces declined. Some split into multiplexes, with floors and walls awkwardly slicing through terra-cotta columns and plaster arches. Others became megachurches. Many were razed. Thankfully, a few have been saved and resurrected as performing-arts centers and theaters, as has been done with the New Amsterdam Theatre in New York, the Oriental Theatre in Chicago, the Franklin Theatre in Franklin, Tenn., the Paramount Theatre in Austin, Texas, and the California Theatre in San Jose.

32. **Mount Rushmore**

TO SOMEONE ARRIVING IN THE Black Hills of South Dakota in the far future, the sight of four gargantuan heads carved into the side of a mountain might seem as unsettling as when George Taylor—the astronaut who fell back to Earth in *Planet of the Apes*—discovers the half-buried Statue of Liberty. This towering monument with George Washington, Thomas Jefferson, Theodore Roosevelt and Abraham Lincoln already seems to be from another time and world; that's what sculptor Gutzon Borglum was striving for. The Paris-trained Borglum believed in working big—what his wife, Elizabeth, said was "the emotional value of volume." He was attracted to the ancient practice of monumental statuary and sanctuaries, and his presidents seem to spring from the mind of the pharaoh Ramses. Borglum created at Mount Rushmore a secular church at which to pay homage to four American heroes, setting them in an open pantheon. To Borglum, the quartet epitomized the first 150 years of the glorious experiment called democracy. When President Calvin Coolidge dedicated the site in October 1927, he said that the monument would be "decidedly American in its conception, in its magnitude, in its meaning and altogether worthy of our country." Work progressed for 14 years, during which laborers blasted, jackhammered and carved away 450,000 tons of granite to reveal the 60-foot-high faces. Completed by Borglum's son, Lincoln, soon after Borglum's death in 1941, Mount Rushmore has appeared often in pop culture and was famously immortalized by Alfred Hitchcock in his vertigo-inducing 1959 film *North by Northwest*. It is one of the most popular park sites in the nation, attracting some 2 million visitors a year.

Louis Sullivan and the Wainwright Building

EXCEPT FOR CHURCHES, there were few tall buildings in America—or, for that matter, anywhere else—prior to the 19th century. Large buildings were load-bearing: the upper floors had to be supported by the lower ones. So the taller a builder went, the wider the base walls needed to be, making true height impractical. That changed with the appearance in the late 19th century of steel skeleton framing, which allowed the frame to support the building. But as a number of early tall buildings went up, they essentially used a babel of architectural motifs; a contemporary guide to Chicago called one building an "Italo-Byzantine-French-Venetian structure with Norman windows." Boston-born architect Louis Sullivan had the vision to realize that these buildings needed the look of a revolutionary form of architecture. As the father of the skyscraper, Sullivan defined what a tall building was: in order to allow a building to visually telegraph its height, he discarded earlier architectural forms, constructing a new vocabulary and, in the process, helped create

architectural modernism. Sullivan conceived of the skyscraper as a column, a tripartite structure with a base, shaft and capital that celebrated its verticality. And instead of using standard classical motifs over the surface, he designed lush geometric and botanically inspired details that he streamed up the brick and terra-cotta sidings. His works were the beginning of artistically designed tall buildings. In a career that spanned five decades, Sullivan, with his partner, Dankmar Adler, created a series of landmark skyscrapers, from the Guaranty Building in Buffalo, N.Y., to his

finest work, the Wainwright Building in St. Louis. Though only 10 stories tall, this tower of Missouri granite, brick, sandstone and terra-cotta [below] beautifully followed the dictum of the man who famously said, "Form follows function." It was, as Sullivan wrote, "every inch a proud and soaring thing, rising in sheer exultation ... from bottom to top." His student Frank Lloyd Wright, who generally had little good to say about other designers, always lovingly called Sullivan "Lieber Meister" and lauded the Wainwright Building as the first structure that was "height triumphant."

VEHICLES AND EXPLORATION

33–34. The Mustang Horse and Car

THE FIRST HORSES ARRIVED EARLY, ON Columbus's second voyage. Others came soon after, as Spanish and other Western explorers, as well as farmers, merchants and missionaries, fanned out across the continent. Some of these horses broke free and became known as mustangs, a staple of the spirit and the land of the West. The wild horse's name is derived from *mustengo*, which in Spanish means "ownerless beast" or "stray horse." As they took to the open fields and plains, breeding at times with quarter and draft horses, the strong, medium-size equines proved ideal for some Native American tribes—so ideal that once those tribes started riding the mustangs, some changed their lifestyles and became nomadic hunters. The horses became a symbol of freedom and a prevalent one: 2 million of them once thundered through the wilds. Now only about 50,000 remain, protected by the Wild Free-Roaming Horses and Burros Act of 1971, their population controlled by the Bureau of Land Management.

Like the horse, the domestically built Mustang car that Ford unharnessed in 1964 wasn't large. Created with the burgeoning baby-boomer market in mind, the automobile was first shown at the New York World's Fair in 1964. Costing $2,368, it sold rapidly, with some 22,000 ordered the first day and 559,451 sold in 1965. The sporty ride, with an image of its namesake adorning its grill, heralded the age of the small "pony cars." Helping to make this one of the coolest and most popular vehicles of the 1960s and '70s was the Mustang's appearance in three James Bond films—*Goldfinger*, *Thunderball* and *Diamonds Are Forever*—as well as the dark green Mustang GT fastback that Steve McQueen drove in *Bullitt* during one of cinema's most famous chase scenes.

35. The Paddle Wheel

A NUMBER OF INVENTORS built boats powered by steam, but it was Robert Fulton who created the first successful steamship. The Pennsylvania-born inventor set an engine onboard the *North River* and placed on the sides of the hull a pair of 15-foot-diameter wheels with evenly arranged horizontal planks that acted as oars. The vessel, which is often called *The Clermont*, took off on its maiden voyage in 1807, ferrying 100 passengers up the Hudson River from New York City to Albany. The trip lasted just 32 hours, compared with the average of four days that a sailing sloop needed to travel that distance. Fulton's ship revolutionized transportation and showed that the steamboat was commercially viable. Others quickly copied and modified his idea. As they did, some set the wheels on the side of their ships, while others placed a large stern wheel out back. Rivers were major natural arteries for travel, and the steamboat easily moved goods and people up- and downstream, reducing the cost of trade. Some of these boats became quite grand, like the show-boats that proliferated in the late 19th and early 20th centuries. These floating palaces contained all that a traveler could need or want: food, saloons, live bands and theater, as well as plenty of friendly, and some not-so-friendly, games of poker.

36. The Prairie Schooner Wagon

AS THE VAST LANDS OF THE CONTINENT were acquired or wrested from France, Britain and Mexico, settlers hankered to move west. In 1841 *New York Tribune* editor Horace Greeley wrote, "Do not lounge in the cities! There is room and health in the country, away from the crowds of idlers and imbeciles. Go west, before you are fitted for no life but that of the factory." As the "Go west, young man" call echoed throughout the East, many men, along with women and children, did just that. But trips along the Oregon and Santa Fe trails were long and at times harrowing. A journey of up to six months was needed to make it across the plains and rivers, over mountains and through passes. The moving van of choice for half a million people was the prairie schooner, essentially a converted farm wagon topped with a white double-ply canvas bonnet stretched over hardwood bows. The shape made it look from a distance like a sailing ship gliding over the prairie's sea of grass. Unlike the heavier Conestoga wagons, which were constructed for freight, the watertight, rectangular-bottomed prairie schooner could ford streams and rivers and float when necessary as it sheltered families along with some 2,000 pounds of essentials, such as cornmeal, flour, sugar, dried fruit and bacon, as well as furniture, rifles and pistols. Settlers even stitched pockets into the overhead canvas for extra storage. The whole caboodle was pulled by teams of oxen, horses or mules. But the ride was rough and jouncy, causing many to prefer to walk alongside or ride a horse. The trip was slow, clocking maybe 20 miles in a day, and was fraught with perils: attacks by American Indians, tramplings by livestock, firearm accidents, and a host of such health concerns as dysentery, cholera and typhoid fever. Yet for those who survived the trek, the prairie schooner delivered to them the chance to set up a new home and put down fresh roots.

37. The Wright Brothers' Plane

WILBUR AND ORVILLE WRIGHT became fascinated with flight when their father, Milton, brought home a small helicopter toy. In 1892 the brothers (Wilbur was older by four years) started a bike shop in their hometown of Dayton, Ohio. As they sold and repaired bicycles, they also read up on glider flight, and, applying their experience with building lightweight vehicles, began some aeronautical tinkering. To test their ideas, in 1900 the brothers went to the town of Kitty Hawk on North Carolina's Outer Banks. There they took advantage of the shore's steady

and brisk winds, open areas and soft terrain on which to land. The locals found them to be pleasant oddities and helped with their glider tests as the brothers obsessively tried to create the first self-propelled aircraft. On Dec. 17, 1903, they prepared *The Flyer*. The contraption [above], with its 12-horsepower, four-cylinder, water-cooled engine, looked like a Tinkertoy agglomeration of sticks and cloth. At about 10:35 a.m., Orville climbed aboard the machine, and as Wilbur ran alongside, the plane rolled down a track and rose into the air. "The machine lifted from the truck just as it was enter-

38. The Indian 101 Scout Motorcycle

NOTHING COMBINES PASSION AND purpose like the Indian motorcycle. This competitor of the better-known Harley-Davidson first took to the road at the same time that the Wright brothers lifted into the air. It has since attracted such rabid fans as James Dean, Steve McQueen and Jay Leno. The firm—the oldest American brand of bike—has built some of the most innovative two-wheeled driving machines. In 1928, Indian's 101 Scout [below], designed by the Irish racer-turned-designer Charles Bayly Franklin and manufactured for three years, fused the id and the ego like no other bike. This sleek yet stripped-down piece of eye candy cradled a 45-cubic-inch, 750cc V-twin engine, making it agile yet powerful, beautiful yet wild. It taunted rivals with what a bike should look and act like. At 370 pounds, it was light, handled well, seemed indestructible— "you can never wear out an Indian Scout," the saying went—and was sought after by city slickers, racers and now collectors eager to straddle its saddle and feel the wind caressing their faces while other bikes follow in their wake.

ing on the fourth rail," Orville wrote shortly thereafter. "I found the control of the front rudder quite difficult on account of its being balanced too near the center and thus had a tendency to turn itself when started so that the rudder was turned too far on one side and then too far on the other. As a result the machine would rise suddenly to about 10 feet and then as suddenly, on turning the rudder, dart for the ground." While *The Flyer* was aloft for a mere 12 seconds and covered just 120 feet on its first flight, that was enough to launch humanity into the age of aviation.

39. **Route 66**

ROUTE 66 IS THE OREGON TRAIL OF highways, a proto-interstate that holds a hallowed place in the land and looms large in the American consciousness. The building of the road began in 1926; it was pieced together from existing national, state and local roads and pitched as "the shortest, best and most scenic route from Chicago through St. Louis to Los Angeles." By 1928, the 2,448-mile route was complete. During the Depression it became what John Steinbeck called "the mother road, the road of flight," as 200,000 "Okies" like the Joad family in *The Grapes of Wrath* fled the barren stretches of the dust bowl for California. Many more travelers passed along Route 66 during World War II seeking jobs in defense plants. With the postwar prosperity and baby boom, families, businessmen and people with a simple wanderlust went westward. They headed to the Grand Canyon and Disneyland, dreamed of breaking into Hollywood or set out in search of themselves, like the "longhaired brokendown hipsters straight off Route 66 from New York" who *On the Road* author Jack Kerouac came across. Along the way, travelers stopped at neon-lit filling stations, mom-and-pop tepee-shaped motels, streamlined moderne diners, drive-in theaters and shops selling "genuine" Native American art. The road was so popular that it inspired musician Bobby Troup to write "(Get Your Kicks on) Route 66," which was recorded by Nat King Cole, the Rolling Stones and others: "Well, if you ever plan to motor west / Just take my way, that's the highway that's the best / Get your kicks on Route 66." With the growth of car culture, President Dwight D. Eisenhower in 1956 started the 42,500-mile interstate highway system. Quickly passed by and passed over by wider, straighter, faster superhighways, Route 66 became a sleepy byway. Yet its path and structures were seen as essential, and in 1999 the National Park Service created the Route 66 Corridor Preservation Program. Today the road, in all its quirky splendor, continues to attract the adventurous traveler.

40. The *Eagle*

ON JULY 20, 1969, AT 4:17 IN THE afternoon—Eastern Daylight Time, planet Earth—Commander Neil A. Armstrong radioed from the moon, "Houston, Tranquillity Base here. The *Eagle* has landed." Early the next day, he stepped out onto the dusty lunar surface, becoming the first human to walk on the moon, and said, "That's one small step for a man, one giant leap for mankind." Nineteen minutes later, Edwin E. "Buzz" Aldrin Jr. joined him, calling the vast plain near the southwestern edge of the Sea of Tranquillity a "magnificent desolation." The two explorers had arrived there aboard the *Eagle*, an ungainly, cubist-like craft that looked like a silver-and-gold-sheathed spider spawned for a 1950s sci-fi film. But this was no B-movie prop; it was a 36,000-pound, 23-by-31-by-31-foot movable, high-tech life station that allowed the astronauts access to an alien surface. There they took photographs, collected rock and soil samples, and set up scientific instruments. They also unveiled a plaque ("Here men from the planet Earth first set foot on the Moon July 1969, A.D. We came in peace for all mankind"), planted an American flag and talked with President Richard Nixon by radio-telephone. After less than 22 hours on the surface, the upper part of the *Eagle* lifted the men off the moon, and they rejoined their colleague Michael Collins, who was orbiting above. Like the *Niña*, *Pinta* and *Santa María*, Christopher Columbus's ships that traveled to America, the fate of this craft is unknown. After docking with the bullet-shaped command module *Columbia*, the *Eagle* was jettisoned into lunar orbit. It is assumed that the ship crashed into the moon within four months.

Henry Ford and the Model T

HENRY FORD HAD A simple dream: "I will build a motor car for the great multitude." He took the Quadricycle, his first horseless carriage, which ran on a two-cylinder, ethanol-powered engine, for a test drive on the streets of Detroit in 1896. Seven years later he incorporated the Ford Motor Company, and in October 1908 he unveiled the Model T. Though small and boxy, the 1,200-pound car—which was said to come in any color as long as it was black—was durable, ran on a 20-horsepower engine, could travel up to 45 miles per hour and was easily repaired. Affectionately called "Tin Lizzie" or the "Flivver," the Model T remained in production from 1908 to 1927, selling more than 15 million in the U.S. and more than a million in Canada and Great Britain. In 1914 Ford Motor's 13,000 workers produced some 300,000 cars, while the other 299 U.S. automakers produced 280,000 combined.

Ford was able to be so prolific through improvements in mass production, and he endeared himself to his workers by paying them a then-generous $5-a-day salary. Further refinements to the assembly-line process allowed him to drop the price of the Model T from the initial $850 to $260 in 1925—essentially democratizing the car by making it available to the common man and woman. Ford's industrial innovations heralded the motor age, the age of movement, which led to the opening up of remote areas and the laying out of the highway system. He set the stage for the creation of the suburbs and an industry that is a pillar of the American and world economies.

INVENTIONS

41–42. The Colt Revolver and the Winchester Rifle

IN THE 19TH CENTURY, PISTOLS AND RIFLES WERE one-shot weapons that needed to be filled with black powder, patch and ball and then tamped down with a ramrod. It could take 20 seconds to load, a long time if you're under attack. But that all changed soon after the Hartford, Conn., native Samuel Colt had a job on a ship. There he became fascinated by the vessel's spinning wheel and wondered about adapting the idea for a pistol. In 1836 he created a multi-chambered weapon, which held half a dozen shots. The gun—the first commercially viable revolving-cylinder firearm—could, according to Colt's patent application, boast "great rapidity in the succession of discharges, which is effected merely by drawing back the hammer and pulling the trigger." Colt's weapons took off when the U.S. Army ordered 1,000 revolvers during the Mexican-American War. And after Colt died in 1862, his company kept innovating, offering in 1873 the Colt Single Action Army handgun. Popularly known as the Peacemaker, the Hogleg and the Equalizer, this .45-caliber weapon was a beautifully balanced six-shooter that became the most famous sidearm of the Wild West, strapped on by Wyatt Earp, Billy the Kid and Rough Rider Theodore Roosevelt. As a Western adage had it, "God created men, and Sam Colt made them equal."

But saying that the Colt .45 was the only gun that "won the West"—well, them's fightin' words. For at around the same time, Boston-born Oliver Winchester got into the weapons business when he bought the Volcanic Repeating Arms Company in New Haven, Conn., and renamed it the Winchester Repeating Arms Company. The factory turned out its 1873 Winchester rifle, a rugged and reliable weapon that smoothly levered the next round of ammo into place. It could be pulled out of a saddle holster for battles with outlaws, cowboys and American Indians as well as with marshals and sheriffs. The rifle was so beloved that there was an expression: "Many a Western baby cut his first teeth on the sling [saddle] ring of a Winchester Model 73 carbine." The weapon became the favorite not only of Texas Rangers but of Buffalo Bill Cody, Butch Cassidy and Pat Garrett. Like the Colt, it helped glamorize and entrench the culture of the gun in the American psyche.

43. **The John Deere Plow**

RUTLAND, VT., NATIVE JOHN DEERE WORKED AS A blacksmith, and in 1836 he moved west, settling in Grand Detour, Ill. While Deere was running his shop, he noticed that cast-iron plows, made for the lighter and sandier soil back east, did not work well in the heavier and stickier prairie-grass-covered sod. As a result, farmers frequently had to stop work to scrape soil off their moldboard. Looking to produce a better plow, Deere took a broken steel saw blade, cut off the teeth, and formed a polished moldboard that sliced clean furrows through soil and roots. His creation initially sold for $10 to $12—an expensive purchase for subsistence farmers at the time—and in 1839 he made only 10 plows. But Deere's design worked well, earning the nickname the "grasshopper plow" because it whisked along like a grasshopper when furrowing the soil. Demand for the implement increased, and in 1842 Deere turned out 100 of them. Then, with a more reliable supply of steel and an 1848 move to Moline, Ill., Deere manufactured 700 plows; by 1857, production hit 10,000. His invention, along with mechanical reapers and threshers by his and other firms, tamed the land, and fields of crops rapidly stretched over the horizon. As the musical *Oklahoma* proclaimed, farmers saw "corn . . . as high as an elephant's eye."

44. The Oil Derrick

PETROLEUM RUNS OUR LIVES, IN THE form of oil for our homes, gas for our cars, fuel for airplanes, asphalt for roads, fabrics for clothes, and plastics for what seems to be everything. And the search for it has shaped the history of our states and nation. In northwestern Pennsylvania in the mid-19th century, oil seeping to the surface was skimmed and collected for medicinal purposes and to light lamps. Investors in the Pennsylvania Rock Oil Company—soon to be renamed the Seneca Oil Company—thought that if they could tap into a deep pool of oil, they could profit handsomely by selling it for lighting. They hired retired railroad conductor Edwin Laurentine Drake to assess the situation; Drake erected a derrick, which supported boring equipment, in Titusville, Pa. In August 1859, Drake drilled down 70 feet and struck black gold. The rush was on, with waves of drillers arriving in search of wealth. The somewhat tent-like derrick that Drake erected evolved into the classic oil derrick: a slender, latticed structure rising above a well. These everyman Eiffel Towers quickly sprouted like trees in oil fields. In 1901, America's first deep oil well gushed at Spindletop, Texas, near Beaumont. The success of that strike ignited a drilling boom, with prospectors erecting towers and eagerly waiting to hear the low rumbling as pressure was released, oil gushed out of the top of the derricks and black crude rained across the land.

45. **Barbed Wire**

WHEN HOMESTEADERS SETTLED THE prairie, they came upon a vast expanse covered by grasses and wildflowers. It was a land bereft of trees or large stones, making it difficult to build fences, let alone homes. Some tried planting rows of bushes and thorny trees to control their livestock, but most just let their animals roam free. With sizable cattle and sheep herds grazing and being driven by ranchers, and with oceans of bison thundering along, farmers needed to protect their crops. Then, at almost the same point in the mid-1870s, Joseph Farwell Glidden, Jacob Haish and Isaac Ellwood each devised ways to attach spiky barbs to a wire. The prickly fencing was the yang to the white picket fence's yin: while the picket fence had a neighborly and welcoming feel that said "Howdy," barbed wire

sharply warned, "Keep out!" Slicing and harsh, it gave homesteaders a way to enclose their land. Others devised their own forms of barbed wire, with more than 500 patents issued from 1868 to 1874. As settlers unrolled fencing and attached it to posts, farming became a more predictable and reliable enterprise. Yet the fencing also adversely affected many. Nomadic Native American tribes, who called it "the Devil's rope," were no longer able to move across the land freely. Ranchers cursed the wire for closing off grazing land. This led to the cutting of wires as well as blood feuds, vigilante justice and range wars. But there was no stopping the division of property. Within two decades, fences enclosed much of the pastureland, ranchers embraced the sharp wire to control their herds, and the native people were resettled.

1870s

1880s

1970s

2010s

46. **The Telephone**

ITS NAME IS ANCIENT, DERIVED FROM THE Greek *téle*, for "far," and *phoné*, for "sound." And that is what the telephone simply does: it allows speech to pass over great distances. People had started to communicate rapidly when Samuel Morse's telegraph arrived in the mid-1830s. With just a series of dots and dashes, Morse code seemed limitless. But the Scottish-born Alexander Graham Bell, a teacher of the deaf, had a bigger idea. While working at the Boston School for Deaf Mutes, Bell became fascinated with the idea of creating a human telegraph. To do this, he needed to send numerous messages over the same wire at the same time. The problem was that telegraphs transmitted over a line using an intermittent current, in which the electrical signal was either on or off, something not conducive to sending sound. Then, in 1874, Bell had the idea of "induced undulating current," which relied on continuous electrical waves. With the goal of creating a "harmonic telegraph," he tried sending sound from one phone to another by setting disks in the receivers. When electrified, the speaking disk would vibrate when spoken into. This vibration would be transmitted to the earpiece in the receiving disk, which would then vibrate in the same way and produce the sound. On March 10, 1876, Bell spoke into the mouthpiece of his device. Downstairs, at the other end, his assistant, Thomas Watson, heard, "Mr. Watson—come here—I want to see you." Watson ran up and said, "I can hear you! I can hear the words!" News of Bell's discovery spread quickly, and he jumped to capitalize on his innovation. In July 1877, the Bell Telephone Company turned out its first phones, and by the end of the year, there were 3,000 phones being used. There would be 10,000 more within another year. Realizing the far-reaching importance of his invention, Bell wrote at the time, "I believe in the future wires will unite the head offices of telephone companies in different cities, and a man in one part of the country may communicate by word of mouth with another in a distant place."

47. The Lightbulb

LIGHT COMES AND GOES WITH THE rising and setting of the sun, and it appears as a faint reflection off the moon. Humans for a long time used candles, oil lamps and fireplaces to see by, but their light was weak and unsteady. What if one could bottle light? That is what Thomas Alva Edison wanted to do. There were lightbulbs before the Wizard of Menlo Park put his mind to the concept, but Edison set out to create a soft, incandescent light that could be used in homes and offices. To do that, he needed just the right long-lasting filament, the material through which electricity flowed and caused the bulb to glow. Edison and his assistants tried whatever they could find to make a filament, from hickory and flax to bamboo and celluloid. "I tested no fewer than 6,000 vegetable growths and ransacked the world for the most suitable filament material," Edison recalled, describing the assortment of substances that failed him. Finally the inventor tried some cotton sewing thread that had been coated with black soot and then baked. Set in a bulb with the air vacuumed out and then filled with an inert gas, the thread heated to an orange glow and continued to give off light for a long period. Once he had produced the light, the question became how to power and distribute it over a wide area. With the help of wealthy financial backers, Edison laid out a square-mile grid of copper wires in lower Manhattan, built six massive electric dynamos and, on Sept. 4, 1882, flipped a switch. Instantly, lightbulbs throughout that part of the city lit up. A *New York Tribune* reporter found a tired but happy Edison at the Pearl Street power station later that evening and commented that "coatless and collarless, though still wearing his white derby hat, the inventor radiated satisfaction over the opening day results."

48. The Brownie Camera

IN THE 19TH CENTURY, PHOTOGRAPHY was a cumbersome business. Photographers lugged around wood-and-brass cameras with large glass plates. The equipment could weigh 50 pounds. George Eastman hoped to simplify the new art form and make it "as convenient as the pencil." In 1888 his Eastman Kodak firm brought out its first portable camera, a small box camera that shot a roll of 100 images. But those cameras were made for a single use, had paper negatives and, at $25 a pop, proved an expensive toy. The following year, Thomas Edison asked Eastman to devise a tough, light and flexible film for his new movie camera, and Eastman created a transparent roll of film that made motion pictures possible. In 1900, Eastman instructed his chief camera designer, Frank Brownell, to fashion an inexpensive camera that worked with the roll of film. The Brownie—represented by a popular illustrated character that Kodak used in advertising—was a simple black box with a viewfinder, a single shutter speed and good depth of field. While unassuming-looking, this compact and sturdy piece of equipment allowed for quick and repetitive picture-making. And at just $1, plus 15 cents for a roll of film, it was an immediate success. Kodak's Rochester, N.Y., factory produced 150,000 cameras the first year, with ads informing parents, "Plant the Brownie acorn and the Kodak oak will grow." But it wasn't just child hobbyists who wanted them. The camera democratized photography by bringing it to the masses. Everyone could now photograph whatever they wanted, whether it was family and friends, landscapes or street scenes. A Brownie took one of the only photos of the sinking of the *Titanic*, and the cameras were packed into the kit bags of soldiers heading off to the front in World War I.

49. The Newsroom

MOST CITIES HAD A TRADITION OF morning, afternoon and evening editions of newspapers. The broadsheets and tabloids were created in newsrooms, noisy places filled with impatient editors, harried reporters and eager copyboys. These spaces reeked of cigarette smoke, the desks littered with cups of coffee and half-eaten sandwiches and staffed by journalists pecking at manual typewriters as they yelled into desk phones. The dogged defenders of the Fourth Estate were overwhelmingly men. They covered fires and scandals and the downfall of a president, with stories that ran under blazing headlines. Some of those stories were noble (MEN WALK ON MOON), others salacious (HEADLESS BODY IN TOPLESS BAR). The image of the newsroom and its inhabitants has been celebrated in film: think of uproarious spoofs like the 1940 *His Girl Friday* and, more recently, of the somber 2015 Academy Award–winning *Spotlight*. Journalism, though, has greatly changed over the past century. Newspapers' daily circulation peaked at 63.3 million in 1984, and the arrival of the Internet and strings of mergers, labor actions and spikes in the cost of paper have buffeted publications and led to a precipitous decline in readership. In 2002, 41% of people polled said they had read a newspaper the previous day. That number plummeted to 23% in 2012. Yet with the rise of the Web, newsrooms have branched out. In the process, journalists have discovered new ways to spread the news, from partnering with filmmakers to posting on Twitter. Many digital start-ups are now set in offices with exposed ductwork or in cavernous industrial spaces, earning revenue through mouse clicks instead of papers sold. Reporters with press cards shoved into their hatbands and steno pads in their hands have been replaced by journalists with Bluetooth earpieces stuck in their ears and digital recorders clutched in their fists. The bastion of maledom is also gone—a third of journalists now are women—and smoking bans are a given, though old coffee and bad food seem to be holdovers from the old days.

50. **The Lipstick Tube**

LIP-COLORING IS AS OLD AS THE PYRA-mids. Cleopatra applied crushed ants and beetles to her lips, while Mesopotamian women spread pulverized semiprecious stones on theirs. Over the centuries, formulas have included olive oil, deer tallow, castor oil and lard. By the 19th century, women had begun to use colors made with red dye mixed with an oil-and-wax base. The concoctions were packaged in silk paper or inserted in a paper tube. Putting them on with a brush, though, could be messy. That the Victorians frowned on cosmetics didn't stop women from wearing them, and suffragettes such as Elizabeth Cady Stanton proudly painted on red lips as a sign of independence. In 1912 the French perfume company Guerlain offered color in a stick form. Three years later, Maurice Levy of Scovil Manufacturing Company in Waterbury, Conn., designed a rugged, bullet-shaped lipstick container that could be slipped into a purse. And to avoid the need for a brush, the nickel-plated item had a slide on the side to cleanly move the stick up or down, allowing for easy application of just the right touch of pizzazz. The growing female workforce embraced the innovation, and within a decade, James Bruce Mason Jr. of Nashville, Tenn., had patented the first swivel-up tube. It is similar to the type produced today in the now $265 billion beauty industry.

51. **The Supermarket**

CUSTOMERS USED TO HAVE TO WAIT patiently at ma-and-pa grocers, butchers and bakers as the clerks picked out and wrapped up their selections. It was time-consuming and expensive. Then, in September 1916, Clarence Saunders of Memphis, Tenn., opened Piggly Wiggly, the first self-service grocery store. With shopping baskets in tow and prices marked on the products, customers could easily pull what they needed from open shelves. By 1923, there were almost 1,300 Piggly Wiggly stores. Others copied his idea, but Michael Cullen thought larger. Much larger. Cullen, who at the time worked for Kroger, envisioned a centrally located store, one that was "monstrous in size" and offered everything you could need. His bosses at Kroger rejected the idea, so Cullen set off on his own and in 1930 opened King Kullen, the first supermarket. Located in Queens, N.Y., the store was promoted by Cullen with the motto "Pile it high. Sell it low." King Kullen quickly attracted shoppers from far and wide, and when Cullen died six years later, the firm had 17 stores. He radically changed how we shop and use our

free time. Many, of course, followed, with chains such as Safeway, ShopRite, Kroger and A&P— the Great Atlantic & Pacific Tea Company— spreading from coast to coast, all offering large varieties and good prices.

52. **The Credit Card**

GOLD AND SILVER HAVE INTRINSIC value. Paper money implies faith in the government. But a 2⅛-by-3⅜-inch plastic card based on the creditworthiness of an unknown bearer takes a real leap of trust. While even children sometimes have one these days, it wasn't that long ago that a credit card was a fanciful idea. In the 1920s some hotels and oil companies gave them to customers to buy their products. Then, in 1946, Charg-It, the first bank card, appeared. It allowed cardholders

with accounts at Brooklyn's Flatbush National Bank to buy from local merchants. In 1950, Diners Club brought out the universal credit card that was accepted at upscale restaurants, and in 1951 Franklin National Bank issued a card that let customers make partial monthly payments. In 1958 American Express offered its card, and the same year what would eventually be known as Visa appeared. A group of banks joined together in the 1960s to form the InterBank Card Association, which later became MasterCard.

This ability to conveniently buy things, though, is a double-edged sword. Although it led to enormous growth of consumer power and fueled the world economy, it also brought with it spiraling debt for many who find the cards all too easy to use. In the U.S., 167 million adults now have at least one credit card, and the nation has the world's highest rate of credit-card debt.

53. Television

ANCIENT GREEK PRIESTS STUDIED BIRD entrails to try to see what the winged creatures saw, and sci-fi characters have communicated with colleagues on distant planets via video monitors. But to most people, the idea of viewing something from far away has been a fantastic and impossible concept. Yet once sound could be transmitted, it was only natural for some scientists to look into capturing and sending images. A long lineage of inventors put their minds to creating what we now know as TV, most notably the Russian-American Vladimir Kosma Zworykin and the Utah-born boy wonder Philo Farnsworth, who figured out how to transmit an image made up of 60 horizontal lines. On April 30, 1939, RCA demonstrated an all-electronic television by broadcasting a speech by President Franklin Roosevelt at the opening of the New York World's Fair. Visitors could watch the transmission on displays set up on the grounds. RCA even included one with a transparent case to show that it was not a gimmick. The following month, RCA's NBC network televised a baseball game for the first time, a matchup between Columbia and Princeton universities, though coverage was limited and the *New York Times* commented that "television is no substitute for being in the bleachers." Things came into sharper focus as broadcast technology improved at the end of World War II. And though there had been television sets around since the 1920s, it was not until 1946 that RCA introduced the first mass-produced unit. Small by modern standards, the 630 TS had a round, 10-inch, black-and-white kinescope screen and came encased in a sleek yet hefty 95-pound mahogany cabinet. Even though it was expensive, at $350, it finally brought television to Americans, who bought more than 200,000 of them by the end of 1947. In no time, the device changed society. By the mid-1950s, more than half of American homes had TV sets, and today at least 116 million households own at least one television.

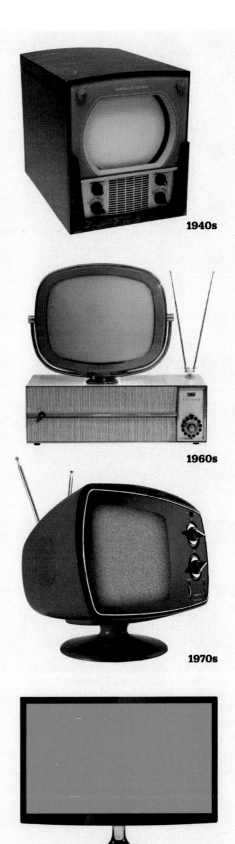

1940s

1960s

1970s

2000s

54. McDonald's Golden Arches

THEY SEEM SO UBIQUITOUS THAT IT IS hard to believe that there was once just one McDonald's. In 1940, Richard and Maurice McDonald opened their McDonald's Bar-B-Q restaurant in San Bernardino, Calif. Soon they renamed it McDonald's Famous Hamburgers and offered 15-cent burgers—"Buy 'em by the bag!"—soft drinks, french fries and shakes. Their success attracted the attention of Ray Kroc, a Chicago-born blender salesman who persuaded the brothers to let him become their franchising agent. The chain swiftly spread, taking on its distinctive look in 1953 when the siblings opened a restaurant in Phoenix set in a red-and-white-tiled building that sported sweeping 25-foot, neon-lit golden arches. Designed by the architect Stanley Clark Meston, the eye-catching spans resembled a large M from certain angles, transforming the building into a roadside sign that alerted drivers that a bite was just up ahead. More McDonald's opened, and by 1958 the chain with the distinctive french-fry-colored arches had sold its 100 millionth burger. Kroc knew a good thing, and in 1961 he bought out the brothers for $2.7 million. He continued to aggressively expand the business, which has since welcomed billions and billions of customers to some 35,000 McDonald's in more than 100 countries.

55. **The Apple II**

IN THE MID-1970S, STEVE WOZNIAK HAD an idea for a microcomputer. But he needed help to make it a reality. Working as an engineering intern at Hewlett-Packard, Wozniak approached his bosses with his idea, but the San Francisco–based firm wasn't interested, so he contacted an old classmate, Steve Jobs. The two set up shop in Jobs's family garage, and to raise money for their tiny company, Apple Computer, Jobs sold his minibus while Wozniak said goodbye to his programmable calculator. Cobbling together loans and arranging credit, they raised enough to create the Apple I and in 1976 sold it at computer stores. But the team didn't want to just make computer kits for geeks. They envisioned a stand-alone machine for the masses. The following year, they brought out the Apple II. With an advanced MOS Technology 6502 chip for its central processing unit and a built-in keyboard, the Apple II came with a total of four kilobytes of memory.

More important, this sleekly designed computer was the first to come in a molded plastic case and could easily be hooked up to a TV or a color monitor, making it a user-friendly system for the average businessperson or student. This was its disarming appeal. It was something that everyone could work and play on and thus became the first commercially successful personal computer. By 1984, the partners had sold more than 2 million Apple IIs, helped start the boom in desktop units and launched the modern computer age.

Benjamin Franklin and His Kite

ELECTRICITY FASCINATED Benjamin Franklin. For besides being a statesman who helped write parts of the Declaration of Independence and the Constitution, he was an avid inventor, creating over his lifetime bifocals, the Franklin stove, the glass harmonica and the odometer. Franklin was especially intrigued by the similarities between electricity and lightning and how they both produced light and made noise. As a result, he became the first scientist to state that lightning *was* electricity. Franklin predicted that his theory could be proved by setting pointed rods on weather vanes or masts

to attract a bolt. He hoped to test his ideas, but there wasn't a building tall enough in Philadelphia for what he wanted to try. French scientists had meanwhile read *Experiments and Observations on Electricity*, the 1751 book containing Franklin's letters on the topic. In May 1752 they attempted his experiment and showed that he was right. Unaware that others had done this, Franklin and his son decided to try a risky test. As a thunderstorm raged in June 1752, Franklin formed a kite with two sticks and a large silk handkerchief and attached to it a line and a key. The kite rose into a cloud, and, sensing that the wet

string had carried down a charge, Franklin touched the key with his knuckle and "perceived a very evident electric spark." He instantly knew that the shock meant that thunderclouds were electrified. But this wasn't the end of his investigation—during his lifetime, Franklin was the first to suggest the use of lightning rods to protect buildings, showed how electricity had a positive and negative charge, defined the distinction between conductors and insulators, created a battery to store electrical charges, and came up with such terms as discharge, charge, condenser, electric shock, electrify and armature.

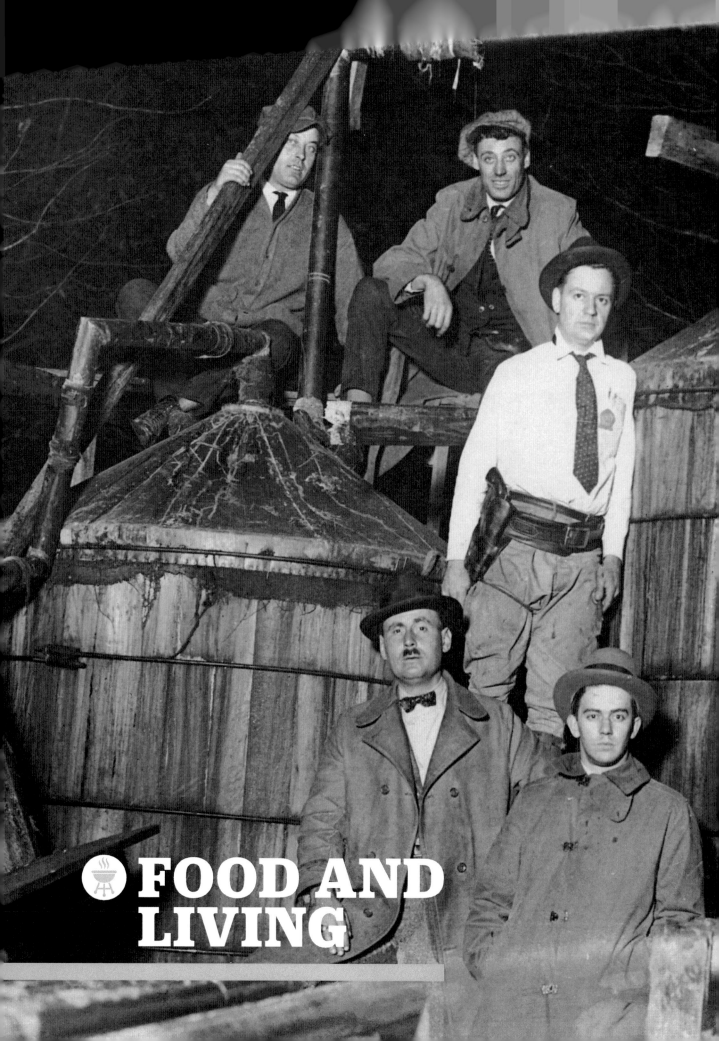

FOOD AND LIVING

56. The Still

THE TERM COMES FROM "DISTILLATION," and in practice it refers to a way to produce hooch with a boiler (to cook the mash) and a condenser (to cool the resulting vapor). However delectable or rotgut the spirits they produce, stills call to mind days of moonshine, illegal backwoods liquor from Appalachia and resistance to government meddling.

The struggle started when President George Washington had to confront armed farmers and distillers opposed to a federal excise tax. To quell the Whiskey Rebellion of the 1790s, the president dispatched Secretary of the Treasury Alexander Hamilton to western Pennsylvania with 12,950 men. As word of their approach spread, the uprising evaporated. Moonshine—which was often produced at night so as not to be discovered—continued to prosper in the South in Virginia, Kentucky and the Carolinas. At the same time that federal revenuers tried to shut down illegal stills, citizens in the 19th and early-20th centuries advocated for the banning of all liquor. As a result, the 18th Amendment to the Constitution was enacted in 1920, prohibiting the manufacture, transportation and sale of intoxicating drink. And while the law mandated a bone-dry land, it created a thriving market for those willing to cook up moonshine, mix batches of bathtub gin and bottle home brew. Stills were in.

Production couldn't keep up with demand, though, leading to the rise of organized crime, as gangsters such as Al Capone, Dutch Schultz and Charles "Lucky" Luciano set the stage for modern crime syndicates. The passage of the 21st Amendment in 1933 ended Prohibition. Even so, 10 states still have dry counties, 15 other counties are partly dry, and there is a thriving market for DIY backyard and countertop stills of varying types and styles, now available through Amazon and deliverable by the U.S. Postal Service.

57. Ketchup

THE AVERAGE AMERICAN CONSUMES more than a pound of ketchup per week—a pound!—slathering it on hamburgers, french fries, hot dogs and eggs. Its name comes from the Hokkien Chinese word *kê-tsiap*, and the puree of tomatoes, peppers, onions, vinegar and spices started as a fermented-soybean-based fish sauce. Dutch and English sailors brought it home in the 17th century, but at the time no one grew soybeans in Europe. Cooks seeking to re-create it tried mixing in oysters, anchovies, elderberries and walnuts. Once ketchup arrived in America, tomatoes were used, and the condiment began being sold in bottles during the 1850s. Its popularity took off after the Civil War, with the *New York Tribune* intoning in 1896 that it sat "on every table in the land." Firms such as Heinz, Hunt's and Del Monte came out with their own versions, and the unrelenting expansion of fast food brought about more varieties. French chefs might scoff at ketchup, but its popularity has spread throughout Europe, South America and Australia—and back to China and the rest of Asia.

58–59. The Potato Chip and the Twinkie

THOMAS JEFFERSON ENJOYED sliced, fried potatoes while in France, so when he was back stateside, he had his chef prepare them. In 1853 George Crum was the cook at Moon's Lake Lodge, a resort in Saratoga Springs, N.Y., where many diners liked the way he prepared his version of those french-fried potatoes. One day, however, a guest complained that the potatoes were too thick. Annoyed by the criticism, Crum sliced some potatoes paper-thin, boiled them in oil and, when they crisped, added salt. Unexpectedly, the guest loved the "crunch potato slices," and Crum's "Saratoga chips" treat soon caught on. They arrived in grocery stores in 1895, offered in barrels or tins. Then, in the 1920s, Laura Scudder was making potato chips at her Monterey Park, Calif., food company. Seeking a way to ensure that her batches lasted longer, she had her workers fashion sealed waxed-paper bags—and in the process changed how goods were sold. Around the same time, Wise Potato Chips in Berwick, Pa., Utz Quality Foods in Hanover, Pa., and Lay's in Dorset, Ohio, started selling their own versions. Today potato chips are a global business, generating several billions of dollars in annual sales.

Another giant among national snack indulgences is the Hostess Twinkie. In 1930 Jimmy Dewar, the manager of Continental Baking Co. in Chicago, was looking for something to take the place of the firm's cream-filled strawberry shortcake when the fruit was out of season. "We needed a good two-pack nickel number," he recalled. Dewar filled some oblong shortcake molds with sponge cake, injected banana filling and dubbed them Twinkies after a nearby billboard for Twinkle Toe Shoes. When bananas became unavailable during World War II, the firm switched to vanilla crème.

Twinkies became a ubiquitous if not-that-healthy pleasure for kids, students and people on the go. They even made their presence known in judicial circles. After Dan White killed San Francisco gay-rights activist and politician Harvey Milk in 1978, White's outlandish defense that eating junk food had led to his murderous ways was roundly derided as the "Twinkie defense." Urban myth also has it that the chemical-infused ingredients of what has been called the "cream puff of the proletariat" could survive a nuclear war. Not true—Twinkies have only a 45-day shelf life.

Twinkies briefly bowed out with the 2012 bankruptcy of food maker Hostess. When word spread of the potential demise, Twinkie junkies rushed out to stockpile boxes. Although production stopped in late 2012, new owners purchased the company, and by the middle of 2013, Twinkies were back on shelves across the country.

60–62. The Tailgate Party, the Barbecue Grill and the Aluminum Can

THERE'S SOMETHING TRIBALISTIC ABOUT a tailgate party, where hundreds of strangers line up their cars, set up portable grills and pop open a few cold ones. It did in fact take a tribe to lay the ground for the phenomenon—specifically, the pre-Columbian Arawak tribe of Hispaniola, who slow-cooked meat over green wood. The Spanish conquistadors liked the smell and taste of what they called *barbakoa* and brought the barbecue style of cooking to mainland America. By the 18th century, those in the Southeast were pit-roasting pigs, and as settlers moved west, different methods of barbecuing evolved. The process was made easier in 1897 when Ellsworth Zwoyer formed charcoal briquettes. And even before Henry Ford's Model T made pulling up to an event easy, tailgating was alive and well. Consider the First Battle of Bull Run, in Prince William County, Virginia, in July 1861. People arrived in stylish carriages and buggies, and women came with carts laden with pies and other foods to sell. "The spectators were all excited," reported a *London Times* correspondent of the battle between the South's Confederates and the North's Yankees, "and a lady with an opera glass who was near me was quite beside herself when an unusually heavy discharge roused the current of her blood—'That is splendid. Oh my! Is not that first rate?' " The North lost that round but scored the decisive win at Appomattox Court House in Virginia in April 1865.

The first football tailgate is thought to have taken place in November 1869, when Rutgers beat neighboring Princeton. And though small and large grills have long been available, the barbecuing set got a real boost from George Stephen of Weber Brothers Metal Works in Chicago, who in 1952 fashioned a dome-shaped grill, which evenly distributes heat and makes one great burger.

Canned beer had been around since 1935, but seven years after Stephen's invention, Coors Brewing Company introduced the first aluminum can, and soon other firms also offered these light, simple-to-transport and rustproof containers. Drinking was made quicker by Ermal Fraze, an Ohio tool manufacturer who devised the pull-tab opener. Then came Daniel Cudzik, an engineer with Reynolds Metals in Richmond, Va., who in 1975 created the safer and less polluting stay-tab. As the planets (and cars) aligned, a tailgate gathering became the perfect spot for people to come together to celebrate a game—whether they actually go inside to watch or not.

63–65. **Meals Made Easy**

NOT THAT LONG AGO, MAKING A MEAL could be a time-consuming process. Many people still had to harvest their own crops and hunt and trap for what they needed before they even entered the kitchen. Three ingenious Americans made food gathering, preparation and eating a lot easier. In Chicago in 1894, Frederick Weeks Wilcox patented a paper "oyster pail" container. Fashioned origami-like from a single piece of paper, it formed a trapezoidal, leakproof, insulated box that vented steam and stayed shut with a simple wire handle. It was used to hold shucked oysters as well as ice cream and other foods. The creation of the box coincided with the rise of Chinese takeout and ensured that your beef and broccoli, Buddha's Delight and steamed rice not only would arrive hot but could also be neatly stored for late-night noshing.

The arrival of grocery stores and supermarkets made getting basic goods easier. But cooks still had to do the often onerous chore of, you know, cooking. New York–born Clarence Birdseye helped provide an alternative. As a fur trader, he had spent time in Labrador, Canada, where he had learned how Eskimos quickly froze fish for the winter. Unlike the slowly chilled food

FROZEN MEALS

CHINESE-TAKEOUT CONTAINERS

that Americans had, the natives' fish tasted good when eaten months later. That's because quickly frozen food does not develop the large ice crystals that ruin cell membranes and degrade texture and flavor. In 1925, Birdseye developed his "quick freeze machine," which chilled food to −40° to −45°F and locked in taste, texture and freshness for vegetables, fruits, fish, meat and even oysters. All one then had to do was heat and eat.

During World War II, William Maxson came up with a better way to feed American troops who were being flown to the front. He created the first frozen meals: an entrée and side dishes set on cardboard trays treated with plastic and frozen to a point at which, as *The New Yorker* commented, "It's as hard as yesterday's dinner rolls and in a state to last until Doomsday at a temperature of zero." At chow time, the on-flight mess staff simply heated the trays in a convection oven called Maxson's Whirlwind. After the war, commercial flights started serving prepared foods, and it was only a matter of time before TV dinners made it into homes across the land, allowing families to sit and eat as they watched episodes of *The Honeymooners*, *Gunsmoke* and *Kukla, Fran and Ollie*.

FROZEN VEGETABLES

66. The Fortune Cookie

NO ONE BELIEVES THAT THE PREDIC-tion sometimes offered in a fortune cookie will come true. But that hasn't stopped those dining in Chinese restaurants (or ordering takeout) from eagerly cracking open the crunchy vanilla-flavored treat at the end of the meal. The cookie, though—like chop suey and General Tso's chicken—is not straight out of China. It was first baked in a California restaurant at the turn of the 20th century. Its origin, like the haiku brevity of its fortune, is most likely the *tsujiura senbei* "fortune crackers" offered at bakeries near a Shinto shrine in Kyoto, Japan. Along with a canned proverb and a brief Chinese-language lesson, most fortune cookies now also contain "lucky" lottery numbers. And for some, their cookies

really have brought fortune. One Tennessee woman in 2005 bought dinner at her favorite Nashville-area restaurant. Her cookie promised, "All the preparation you've done will finally be paying off." It seemed to bode well, so she bought a Powerball ticket using the numbers included, and she won. She was not the only one to receive that fortune and buy a ticket. An unprecedented 110 people split the second prize for the $19.4 million jackpot drawing, each taking home $100,000 to $500,000. When officials looked into the suspiciously high number of winners, they discovered that many of them had played the cookie-sent numbers, which originated at Wonton Food, a bakery in Queens, N.Y. As one of that company's sales executives said, "Those people are very, very lucky."

67. **The Coca-Cola Bottle**

IN 1886, ATLANTA PHARMACIST JOHN PEMBERTON CONCOCTED A flavored syrup that, when mixed with carbonated soda, made a refreshing, fizzy drink. Asa Candler bought his formula in 1888, but at the time, five-cent glasses of Coca-Cola could be enjoyed only at soda fountains. A few years later, Joseph Whitehead, Benjamin Thomas and John Lupton acquired the bottling rights and filled straight-sided bottles with the stuff. But success breeds imitation, and competitors with suspiciously similar products, such as Toka-Cola and Koka-Nola, replete with knockoff logos, marketed their beverages. Needing to set its drink apart, the Coca-Cola Bottling Association asked its numerous glass companies to create a unique bottle. The Root Glass Company in Terre Haute, Ind., proposed an easy-to-grasp bottle based on the elongated shape of a cocoa bean, complete with the seed's rippling ribs. The company patented the design and decided to have it colored what became known as "Georgia green" in homage to its home state. The bottle came out in 1916 and was an immediate hit, with six-packs appearing in 1923. It has such a distinctive shape—one that could even be recognized by touch in the dark— that after its patent expired in 1977, the U.S. Patent and Trademark Office issued the company a rare trademark registration for its package. The famed industrial designer Raymond Loewy crowed that the bottle was the "perfect liquid wrapper," and such artists as Salvador Dalí, Robert Rauschenberg and Andy Warhol have celebrated it in their art. Its fame has lasted longer than a Warholian 15 minutes: although the drink is now available in cans and containers of various shapes and sizes, many of the 1.9 billion servings sold each day are still quaffed from the traditional bottle formed a century ago.

68. **K-Rations**

OK, IT WASN'T YOUR MOTHER'S HOME cooking. But at least your folks knew that while you were fighting in World War II, the Army quartermaster gave you three squares a day. And though pre-packaged meals existed before the war, the Army, aware that soldiers hated them, sought to improve the fare for the troops. So the service asked physiologist Ancel Benjamin Keys to create a lightweight yet nutritious meal that could be carried by bailing paratroopers. What he put together was the K-ration. It came in a wax-coated cardboard box with three separate meals of concentrated or dehydrated food, cereal, crackers, bouillon powder, potted meat and the ever popular Beech-Nut chewing gum and Chesterfield cigarettes. The food weighed just 28 ounces but was packed with some 3,000 calories. And even if Mom would have made something a lot tastier, K-rations worked well for the millions off at war. The gum was especially loved by the children of the liberated lands, who followed troops with the hope of being handed a treat. By the end of the war, the U.S. Army had distributed 105 million K-rations.

69. The Drive-Through Window

ON-THE-GO FOOD PLACES HAVE existed since the 1920s, but it took car culture to really get the phenomenon rolling. By World War II, carhop service was common at drive-up restaurants offering fare such as burgers and ice cream

floats, some brought out by roller-skating waitresses. In 1947, Red's Giant Hamburg in Springfield, Mo., opened the first drive-through. No longer did time-obsessed diners need to walk into a restaurant or pull up and wait to be served. The idea exploded, with customers gliding into designated lanes, choosing their selections from a large placard, placing their order by speaking into a two-way speaker and then picking up their bagged meal; In-N-Out Burger also gave customers a sheet of butcher paper to protect their laps while they ate. By the 1980s, fast-food chains reported that 50% of their business came through the windows. Some companies devised products that could be held in one hand while the other clutched the wheel.

But it isn't just food that people like to pick up without leaving their cars. There are now drive-through banks, pharmacies, liquor stores and bars (maybe not a good idea), voting booths, law firms and emergency rooms. There are wedding chapels for tying the knot on the go—and even funeral parlors, where the bereaved can view their departed loved ones, thus making us all the more rushed in love and death.

Julia Child and Fine Food

A T SIX FOOT TWO INCHES tall, Julia Child was a towering presence. But there was something down-to-earth about the chef born in Pasadena, Calif. Child originally took cooking classes in Los Angeles to prepare for married life, though her husband Paul admitted that at first she wouldn't have been *Michelin Guide*–worthy: "I was willing to put up with that awful cooking to get Julia," he said. They settled in Paris, where Child fell in love with French cuisine, studied the techniques and co-founded a cooking school. But a classroom could not contain the effusive chef and her desire to spread her passion. In 1961 she came out with *Mastering the Art of French Cooking*, a best seller that led to her immensely popular TV cooking show, *The French Chef*. Through the show—and such

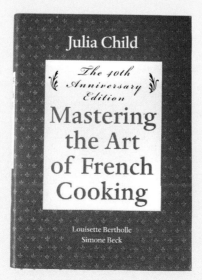

subsequent programs as *In Julia's Kitchen with Master Chefs*—her enthusiasm for fine food, delivered in her otherworldly warbly voice, was beamed into homes across America. Child combined an

encyclopedic knowledge of haute cuisine with an utter lack of pretension, as well as a quick wit. She cooked and baked with aplomb, owned up to her culinary faux pas and made everyone feel they had a station in her kitchen and a seat at her table. Advising readers and viewers to "be fearless, and above all have fun," she helped transform a nation that once seemed to subsist on meat, potatoes and rye whiskey into a land of foodies who relish ratatouille, boeuf bourguignon and French onion soup as they search for rare truffles and brawny wine. Child's pioneering cooking and TV style have been embraced by a generation of on-air cooks. Child, though, was and forever will be the executive chef in our nation's kitchen, a gracious hostess always wishing us a fond *"Bon appétit!"*

67

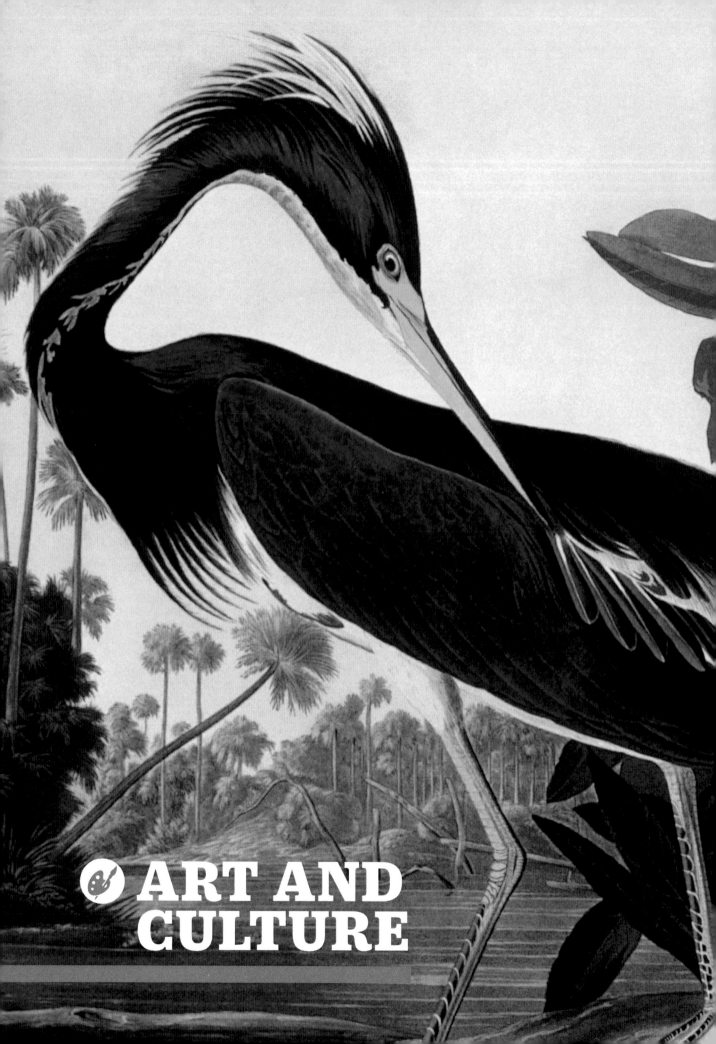

ART AND
CULTURE

70. *Birds of America*

BIRDS WERE JOHN JAMES AUDUBON'S passion. In the 1830s and '40s he spent long stretches in the wild living off the land so he could observe and study them. He took notes on their habits and habitats, and he also shot some of them so he could set them in lifelike poses on wooded and wire armatures and accurately illustrate them. Audubon's sharp focus led critic Lewis Mumford to call him "an archetypal American who astonishingly combined in equal measure the virtues of George Washington, Daniel Boone and Benjamin Franklin." Audubon hoped to create "a collection of the Birds of our Country, from Nature, all of Natural Size." But he had no backers in America, so he headed to England. There he exhibited his paintings and found patrons. In order to inspire subscribers for his grand set of engravings, he attended European salons dressed in a bearskin cloak to come across as a rugged woodsman.

And still Audubon continued to trudge into the wilderness in search of subjects, making his way from the tip of the Florida Keys to Labrador, Canada, from New York to Wyoming. It took printers from 1827 to 1838 to complete his collection. Audubon's 435 hand-colored engravings celebrated 1,055 birds, including 25 new species and 12 subspecies. This wasn't simply an analytical collection with pretty pictures like those offered by other artists. It was a monumental work of art and literature, presenting rich, detailed and vibrant images of life-size creatures. He portrayed a wild turkey strutting, a common buzzard swooping down onto a hare and a Louisiana heron casually grooming its plume [left]. Every few months, subscribers received a package of five 26½-by-39½-inch prints, which they could gather into bound volumes known as the Double Elephant Folios. As a historical record, Audubon's *Birds of America* is quite valuable: it contains a number of species that are now extinct, such as the Labrador duck and the Carolina parakeet—along with the carbonated warbler, whose existence, Audubon's art notwithstanding, has never been confirmed.

71. *Uncle Tom's Cabin*

HARRIET BEECHER STOWE WAS BORN into an American dynasty, the seventh of 13 children of the famed minister Lyman Beecher. All of her brothers became ministers, including Henry, a fiery anti-slavery advocate. Harriet's oldest sister, Catharine, was a respected educator, and her youngest sister, Isabella, helped found the New England Woman Suffrage Association. After Stowe's family settled in Cincinnati in 1832, Harriet began to learn more about slave society. She gathered freedom narratives and helped runaways. She moved to Brunswick, Maine, just as Congress passed the Compromise of 1850. That law included the much-hated Fugitive Slave Law, which required people to help recapture runaway slaves. When the editor of the abolitionist newspaper *The National Era* approached Stowe about creating a story that would "paint a word picture of slavery," she took to writing with the fervor of a revival minister. As she later recalled, "I wrote what I did because as a woman, as a mother, I was oppressed and brokenhearted with the sorrows and injustice I saw, because as a Christian I felt the dishonor to Christianity—because as a lover of my country, I trembled at the coming day of wrath." Stowe's story about the saintly slave Uncle Tom, who is killed because of his refusal to inform on runaways, put a face to slavery, embarrassed polite society, galvanized abolitionists and terrified slave owners. Gathered together in 1852 as *Uncle Tom's Cabin; or, Life Among the Lowly*, the book sold 300,000 copies its first year. Some historians say it also helped set off the Civil War. Upon meeting Stowe in 1862 at the White House, President Abraham Lincoln reportedly said to her, "So you're the little woman who wrote the book that started this great war."

SOLID COMFORT

72. *The Adventures of Huckleberry Finn*

HUCKLEBERRY FINN IS AN UNLIKELY hero. He is a poor delinquent from the wrong side of the river who finally feels "mighty free and easy and comfortable on a raft" as he floats down the Mississippi. And particularly shocking for those picking up a copy of *The Adventures of Huckleberry Finn* in 1885 was that Huck's friend and companion, Jim, was a runaway slave. The book, something of a sequel to Mark Twain's 1876 *The Adventures of Tom Sawyer*, paints a vivid picture of pre–Civil War America, of class distinction, the horrors of slavery and Jim's trek to freedom. But what made Twain's work so groundbreaking was its use of vernacular dialogue, the voices of African Americans, and its portrayal of how Huck sees beyond Jim's color and protects his friend. Ernest Hemingway said, "All modern American literature comes from one book by Mark Twain called *Huckle-*

berry Finn." Yet the crassness of the characters, the unschooled nature of Huck and the blatantly incorrect designation of *Huckleberry Finn* as a racist work because of its use of language have shrouded Twain's masterpiece in unwarranted controversy and led to the banning of the book. The year of its publication, the library in Concord, Mass., called it "suitable only for the slums." Since then, some schools across the country have removed it from reading lists, and by the mid-1990s, the nonprofit People for the American Way listed it as the most frequently challenged book. Often missed in the controversy is how Twain's antislavery book was written in the context of its age. Through the unschooled Huck, Twain unleashed a scathing assault on the hypocrisy of a seemingly high-minded democracy that condoned the brutalization of men, women and children.

73. *The Broncho Buster*

FREDERIC REMINGTON, BORN IN canton, N.Y., grew up after the Civil War, at a time when, as the historian Frederick Jackson Turner intoned, "The frontier has gone." Yet for Remington, the past was present, and after visiting Montana in 1881 he set out to explore that world. For him, the frontier was a living, breathing space with vast plains, crusty cattlemen, dusty soldiers and determined Native Americans. As Remington wandered west of the Mississippi, he made copious drawings and photographs of life outdoors. He then brought his work back to his Brooklyn studio, where he created art that celebrated the rough-and-ready drama of the people and the region. In the process, he shaped our perception of the old West. The accuracy of Remington's work, along with his lack of condescension toward the inhabitants, captivated readers of publications such as *Harper's Weekly, Collier's, Outing, Boys' Life* and *Cosmopolitan*. One piece he created, to accompany an article written by Theodore Roosevelt for *Century* magazine in 1888, was of a bronco buster attempting to tame a horse. (The future president owned a cattle ranch in the Dakota Territory.) In 1895 Remington started what would be a series of 22 bronze statues that epitomized the West. The first and most famous is *The Broncho Buster*. Adapted from his drawing *Pitching Broncho*, which appeared in *Harper's* three years earlier, it shows a cowboy trying to break a rearing horse and freezes the animal's violent jerking and leaping, along with the rider's determination to stay on despite what Remington called "the sky-rocket bounds, grunts and stiff-legged striking." After Roosevelt returned from the 1898 Spanish-American War, his Rough Riders cavalry presented their lieutenant colonel with a cast of *The Broncho Buster*. Roosevelt was so moved by the sculpture that he told his men the gift "is something I shall hand down to my children, and I shall value it more than I do the weapons I carried through the campaign." Roosevelt proudly displayed the statue over the fireplace in his home in Oyster Bay, N.Y.

74–75. Ragtime and Rap

THERE'S SOMETHING JAUNTILY MODern about ragtime, a syncopated music that swept across America before World War I. It joyously combines European classical styles with American marches, black banjo music and minstrel songs. The undisputed king of ragtime was Scott Joplin, the Texas-born son of a freed slave who, in 1899, brought out the "Maple Leaf Rag." Joplin had a preternatural melodic and compositional sense, and his pieces possess what he called a "weird and intoxicating" rhythmic feel. While polite white society frowned upon ragtime as immoral—the music monthly *The Etude* called it "virulent poison"—Joplin boasted that "ragtime is an invention that is here to stay." The "Maple Leaf Rag" set off a craze for ragtime. It helped boost piano sales, flooded America and Europe with songs and piano rolls, and made the "Maple Leaf Rag" the first piece of instrumental sheet music to sell a million copies. More than that, Joplin had grand plans for rags, which he called American classical music. He wanted the style to be taken more seriously than just as popular fare and hoped that his and others' creations would show proper society that black composers were the equal of white composers. Yet Joplin, who died in 1917 at age 49, did not live to see his wish come true. And while such composers as Igor Stravinsky and George Gershwin found inspiration in ragtime, the style quickly faded, supplanted by jazz, stride piano, boogie-woogie and other musical forms. It wasn't until the film *The Sting* appeared in 1973 and featured the music of Joplin that ragtime earned a revival and a higher level of respect. Three years later, *Treemonisha*—Joplin's never fully staged opera masterwork—appeared, and he won a Pulitzer Prize for his contributions to American music.

Rap music has a similarly propulsive drive. Born in the early 1970s in black communities in the Bronx, Brooklyn and Queens, it was performed in discos and at parties where dueling rappers improvised mind- and tongue-twisting rhymes. Sylvia Robinson and her husband ran the All Platinum label, and she first heard the music at a birthday party in Harlem in 1979. Realizing its possibilities, she and her son Joey brought together rappers Henry "Big Bank Hank" Jackson, Guy "Master Gee" O'Brien and Michael "Wonder Mike" Wright. In one 15-minute take, the newly dubbed Sugarhill Gang good-naturedly unspooled "Rapper's Delight" over Chic's R&B hit tune "Good Times." Released on Robinson's new Sugar Hill label, "Rapper's Delight" was picked up by mainstream radio and introduced the music to white listeners. The following January, it hit No. 36 on the pop chart, becoming the first rap song to make it into the U.S. top 40. Other labels started recording rap, and the art form soon overwhelmed the musical floodgates. As Joey Robinson recalled, "We recorded it for $700. It paved the way for a multibillion-dollar industry and a whole new genre of music."

SCOTT JOPLIN'S
"MAPLE LEAF RAG"

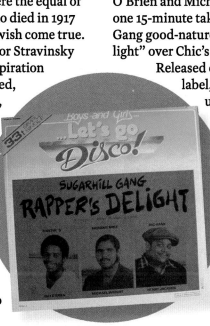

SUGARHILL GANG'S
"RAPPER'S DELIGHT"

76. Tiffany's Dragonfly Lamp

THE SON OF THE MERCHANT WHO founded the famed jewelry store, Louis Comfort Tiffany grew up surrounded by luxury. He began as a landscape painter and ended up designing a vast array of work: jewelry, pottery, metalwork, mosaics, enamels and more. In 1875 he started investigating the possibilities of stained glass. When he redecorated the White House in 1883 for President Chester A. Arthur, Tiffany installed a translucent foyer partition in the entrance hall made up of eye-popping crimson, cobalt, white, blue-white, rosy-white and amber-white glass panels. As he experimented with new ideas, Tiffany developed a range of leaded glass—marbleized, opalescent, Favrile, volcanic and confetti—in pieces that shimmered, rippled and shifted colors depending on how they were looked at. The resulting lamps, windows and vases became wildly popular. Many of the pieces were created by a team of female designers dubbed the Tiffany Girls, a group that the

New York Daily News in 1904 called "the only shop of women glass cutters in the world." Clara Wolcott Driscoll headed the artisans, who designed the firm's most famous lamps, layering on images of fruits and flowers and insects. The pieces of glass were of different thicknesses so as to enhance the play of light, causing the cobwebs, butterflies and wisteria to glow and seem to move.

The most beautiful of these creations was the dragonfly lamp. Translucent four-winged insects encircle the shade's rim and seem to hover above a pool of water. In 1900 the lamp won Driscoll the bronze medal at the Paris World's Fair. In 1906 the lamps could be purchased for $175 each, quite a lot when the average hourly wage was 17½ cents and Driscoll made about $35 a week. Do they still have value? At an auction in 2015, one such lamp sold for $2.1 million.

77. Louis Armstrong's Cornet

LOUIS "SATCHMO" ARMSTRONG KNEW how to blow a horn, but his childhood gave no clue that he would someday become one of the greatest jazz musicians ever. Growing up in New Orleans when jazz was young, he could hear music wafting from local dance halls and bars, and he sang in a boys' quartet. After being arrested at age 11 for shooting a pistol to celebrate New Year's Eve, he landed in the Colored Waifs' Home for Boys, a reform school. He came under the tutelage of the home's band director, Peter Davis, who gave him lessons on the cornet. Music became Armstrong's passion, and when he emerged in 1914, he bought his first cornet at a pawnshop. It cost $10, and he recalled how it was "all bent up, holes knocked in the bell." Even so, he mastered the horn's mellow sound, and with new and better instruments he played in local honky-tonks, for marching and jazz bands, and then on Mississippi riverboats. Armstrong, with his large range, astonishing technique and daring harmony, was much in demand. In 1922 he headed to Chicago and soon after to New York, where his energetic playing roused audiences. By the mid-1920s, he had recorded classic records with the Armstrong Hot Five and Hot Seven groups and become a renowned instrumentalist, with pieces like "Potato Head Blues." He helped invent scat singing and influenced many, including Coleman Hawkins, Bing Crosby and Billie Holiday. Though he played on many cornets and trumpets during his career, he favored the Conn Peashooter cornet and the Selmer trumpet as he toured America and Europe and recorded the works of Hoagy Carmichael, Duke Ellington and Irving Berlin.

78. *Joy of Cooking*

NOT THAT LONG AGO, THE idea of a book devoted solely to recipes was hard to conceive. When Fannie Farmer's *The Boston Cooking-School Cook Book* appeared in 1896, Farmer promised readers that her book "may awaken an interest through its condensed scientific knowledge which will lead to deeper thought and broader study of what to eat." She offered ways to make offerings like "after-dinner coffee" and the puff pastry Zigaras à la Russe. In 1901 Lizzie Kander brought out her *Settlement Cookbook*, combining recipes for scrambled eggs and fondue bourguignonne with tips on how to keep a house clean and store food. But most cookbooks were, as the critic H.L. Mencken said, put together by "cooking-school marms" or "a vast and cocksure rabble of dietitians." In 1930 Irma S. Rombauer started to amass her favorite recipes in *Joy of Cooking*. Now in its ninth edition, the book has sold more than 18 million copies and become the most popular cookbook in America. It is a readable, accessible yet encyclopedic compilation of life in the kitchen. The book's dog-eared and sauce-stained pages are tapped by the novice and the expert alike hoping to tackle a range of foods and treats. Pancakes and spaghetti, a bûche de Noël yule-log cake, pan-roasted venison loin wrapped in ramps and bacon—they're all there. Others followed Rombauer's lead, with *Betty Crocker's Picture Cook Book* becoming a best seller in 1950. In the current age of cooking shows, a self-written cookbook seems as de rigueur for every host chef as a saucepan and whisk.

79. *American Gothic*

GRANT WOOD STARTED OUT AS AN Impressionist painter, but during a time in Germany in the late 1920s, he fell under the spell of the deeply detailed realism of 16th-century Flemish and German artists. After returning home to Iowa, he came across a simple Carpenter Gothic–style farmhouse in the town of Eldon. Wood later recalled, "I imagined American Gothic people with their faces stretched out long to go with this American Gothic house." Wood had his sister, Nan Wood Graham, and his dentist, B.H. McKeeby, dress as if they were "tintypes from my old family album" and posed them in front of the 1880 house. The rigid formality of this impeccable antimodernist creation possesses a hint of medieval influence, while the starkness of the characters and setting mirrors the straitlaced American farmers who worked in the heartland. The painting caused a sensation when it appeared in a competition at the Art Institute of Chicago in 1930, winning Wood a $300 prize. More important, it made Wood a leader of art's anticosmopolitan Regionalist movement, which included such artists as Thomas Hart Benton and John Steuart Curry. Yet *American Gothic* has always been elusive, especially the relationship between the pair: a pitchfork-clutching husband and his wife or a stern father and spinster daughter? It has inspired countless theories about its meaning, just like Leonardo da Vinci's *Mona Lisa*, with her mysterious smile, and the otherworldly rage in Edvard Munch's *The Scream*. *American Gothic* has been parodied in various media (including *The Simpsons*), and Nan regularly sued those who she felt improperly referenced her brother's masterpiece.

80–81. **Superman and Batman**

SUPERMAN FIRST LANDED ON EARTH IN 1938. Created by artists Jerry Siegel and Joseph Shuster—who sold their idea to Action Comics for $130—"The Man of Steel" is an orphaned child named Kal-El who is taken from the dying planet Krypton. He arrives here "with power and abilities far beyond those of mortal men," which include an absurdly high level of strength and the ability to fly. Yet growing up as Clark Kent in rural Kansas, this immigrant keeps his ancestry a secret so he can work at the *Daily Planet*, a "great American newspaper." From his journalist perch in urban Metropolis, Kent fights for "truth, justice and the American way." And there is much battling as he works to keep his adopted home planet—and especially his friends Lois Lane and Jimmy Olsen—safe from enemies foreign, domestic and alien.

One year after Superman arrived, a darker and more tortured character flapped off the comic boards and roosted on America's newsstands. Created by Bob Kane and Bill Finger for rival DC Comics, Batman is the alter ego of Bruce Wayne, a child of wealth whose early trauma of seeing his parents murdered causes him to spend "the rest of my life warring on all criminals." While the Caped Crusader lacks Superman's Olympian abilities, he confounds criminals with science and American know-how. This includes an arsenal of curious gadgets with which to battle Gotham City's cartoonish array of riddling, freezing and bird-faced villains. Many of Batman's crime-fighting contraptions are ingenious; the Joker in the 1989 film *Batman* wondered, "Where does he get those wonderful toys?" Both Batman, at times with his sidekick Robin [left], and Superman have spawned huge movie franchises, and they recently teamed up in *Batman v Superman: Dawn of Justice* to keep us all safe.

82. *The Wizard of Oz*

L. FRANK BAUM'S MOST FAMOUS BOOK FROM HIS Oz series follows young Dorothy and her little dog, Toto, as they try to return home to their hardscrabble life in Kansas. The place they hope to escape from is surreal and threatening, populated with witches, chatting trees, flying monkeys, Munchkins and a man behind a curtain. Along the way, the pair are befriended by an unlikely troika of friends: the daffy Scarecrow, the heart-seeking Tin Woodman and the Cowardly Lion. It is a story made for the big screen. Silent versions appeared before World War I, and the success of Disney's 1937 film *Snow White and the Seven Dwarfs* inspired MGM to not just make a movie but find a way to tell the story on a scale never before seen. While most films then were still made in black and white, the studio sought to saturate its live-action movie with color. Costume and scenery designers made a rainbow palette an integral part of the story: when captured in Technicolor, the film showed the stark difference between monochromatic Kansas and the proto-psychedelic Land of Oz. But though *The Wizard of Oz* won two Oscars and made a star of Judy Garland, the 1939 film—with some 600 actors, almost 1,000 costumes and a massive electric bill—was a box-office disappointment. It cost a then-whopping $2.8 million and initially pulled in only $3 million. It wasn't until it arrived on television that it became a popular mainstay. According to the Library of Congress, it is now the most-watched movie in history.

83–84. *Playboy* and *The Feminine Mystique*

IN THE VERY FIRST ISSUE OF *PLAYBOY*, in 1953, founder Hugh Hefner promoted its philosophy: "If you're a man between the ages of 18 and 80, *Playboy* is meant for you. We enjoy mixing up cocktails and an hors d'oeuvre or two, putting a little mood music on the phonograph, and inviting in a female acquaintance for a quiet discussion on Picasso, Nietzsche, jazz, sex . . ." The magazine was immensely successful. Many American men embraced the *Playboy* lifestyle and promoted the *Mad Men*–ish belief that they should have freedom in everything. Over the years, Hefner persuaded stars such as Ursula Andress, Kim Basinger and Pamela Anderson to strip for *Playboy*'s cameras. But wanting more than just a girlie magazine, he elevated *Playboy* by including works by heavyweight authors such as Joseph Heller, Margaret Atwood and Gabriel García Márquez, as well as thought-provoking interviews with societal forces such as Vladimir Nabokov, Martin Luther King Jr., the Beatles and Fidel Castro. Through growing competition and new technology, however, the revolution that the magazine created toppled its creator. Circulation dropped, from 5.6 million in 1975 to about 800,000 now. In 2016 it stopped publishing naked images of women.

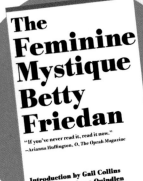

As Playboy Enterprises CEO Scott Flanders said, "You're now one click away from every sex act imaginable for free. And so it's just passé at this juncture."

While Hefner saw women as toys, Betty Friedan believed they had vast, untapped potential. Friedan, who spent a decade as a housewife in suburban New York, knew there was no mystique to being a woman in post–World War II America and of the challenges in the nurturing sanctity of marriage, child-rearing and housework. Seeking to understand the state of modern women, Friedan interviewed her Smith College classmates, and in 1963 she released her landmark *The Feminine Mystique*. In it, she stressed how women dreaded their stifling roles—what she called "the problem that has no name"—and explored how the emphasis on marriage and the discouragement from higher education forced women to seek fulfillment through their families. Friedan said women could find personal and professional success by pursing college and a career. Her work jolted the nascent women's movement, causing women to reappraise their position in society. Three years later, she co-founded the National Organization for Women, which for the past half-century has fought for women's rights and equality. Generations of women have taken Friedan's message to heart: in 1963, only 38% of women worked, but in 2012, 58% did; in 1962, just 6.7% of women completed at least four years of college, but in 2011 that number reached 32%.

85. **Warhol's *Campbell's Soup Cans***

EVEN BEFORE ANDY WARHOL FOUNDED his Factory in New York, with its mirrors, aluminum paint and odd assortment of occupants, there was already an industrial quality to much of his work. Making a living as a successful commercial illustrator, Warhol embraced the mass production of art, fashioning pieces that looked as if they had rolled off a conveyor belt. In the early 1960s he was inspired by ads and comics and started to make his first Pop paintings. When a friend suggested that he create something everyone recognized, Warhol thought of how much he enjoyed Campbell's soup. "I used to drink it," he recalled. "I used to have the same lunch every day, for 20 years." Warhol bought some cans and reproduced their images over and over again with assembly-line precision, giving them the mass-produced feel of a piece of advertising. Each of Warhol's 32 *Campbell's Soup Cans* paintings corresponds to one variety of the brand's soup and sports the golden fleur-de-lis

pattern that rings the product's bottom. The seemingly mundane yet revolutionary collection first appeared at Los Angeles's Ferus Gallery, where, like the actual store-bought soup cans, the artworks were lined up along a shelf. The show was unexpected, original and perplexing, causing a competing gallery to make fun of it by exhibiting a stack of cans, which it sold for two for 33 cents. Yet Warhol's cans would prove a much better investment; collectors such as actor Dennis Hopper bought the work. Then, realizing that the paintings should be kept together, gallery owner Irving Blum repurchased them. In 1996 New York's Museum of Modern Art bought the group from Blum for $15 million. The simple soup can with the red-and-white label made Warhol a celebrity. For an artist who produced a vast array of work, these paintings became his favorites. "I should have just done the *Campbell's Soups* and kept on doing them," he said, "because everybody only does one painting anyway."

86. "Letter from Birmingham Jail"

IN APRIL 1963, THE YOUNG MINISTER Martin Luther King Jr. and his Southern Christian Leadership Conference turned their focus to Birmingham, Ala., in an attempt to end that city's segregation in hiring and at lunch counters. King's followers and the Alabama Christian Movement for Human Rights held peaceful mass meetings, organized marches and sat in at lunch counters. But King and his activists came up against Theophilus Eugene "Bull" Connor, the ultra-segregationist commissioner of public safety who believed in blunt-force justice and the quick arrest of protesters. Nonetheless, King continued demonstrating, declaring, "I have to make a faith act." On Good Friday, the police clapped him into solitary confinement. There, King started to write in the margins of the *Birmingham News* his "Letter from Birmingham Jail," noting, "What else can one do when he is alone in a narrow jail cell, other than write long letters, think long thoughts and pray long prayers?" King wrote how he came to Birmingham "because injustice is here," and he spelled out his hope that his group's action would "create a situation so crisis packed that it will inevitably open the door to negotiation."

The time for waiting for society to change, he wrote, had passed: "For years now I have heard the word 'Wait!' It rings in the ear of every Negro with piercing familiarity. This 'Wait' has almost always meant 'Never.' "

After eight days, under pressure from John F. Kennedy's administration, the city released the civil rights leader. But the protests continued. Stunned Americans watched on the news as police sicced their dogs on demonstrators, clubbed schoolchildren and unleashed torrents of water from high-pressure fire hoses. In response, Kennedy sent in federal troops to restore calm, and on June 11 the president announced his plan to propose civil rights legislation to Congress. Meanwhile, King's supporters made mimeograph copies of his epistle—with memorable lines such as "Injustice anywhere is a threat to justice everywhere." His message soon appeared in magazines and newspapers, and that August he led the March on Washington, where he spoke of his dream for a better America. The following July, President Lyndon B. Johnson signed the Civil Rights Act, which prohibited discrimination in public places. That October, the Nobel Committee awarded King its peace prize.

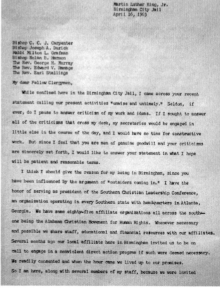

Georgia O'Keeffe and Her Flower Paintings

GEORGIA O'KEEFFE SAW beauty in overlooked things. She collected seashells, skulls and rocks and observed that "to see takes time, like to have a friend takes time." O'Keeffe first learned to look closely as a teenager, discovering the beauty of the world in a single flower. While she was at school in Sun Prairie, Wis., an art teacher introduced her to jack-in-the-pulpit, a late-summer, glossy, large-leaved woodland plant with a hooded vase-shaped flower and a bright cluster of red berries.

O'Keeffe later recalled, "This was the first time I remember examining a flower . . . she started me looking at things—looking very carefully at details." Her intense focus stayed with her throughout her life. In the 1920s she began rendering images of flowers on a large scale, believing it would cause "even busy New Yorkers" to stop and reflect on them. She not only elevated everyday objects to high art; she made people see them in a new way. O'Keeffe said, "When you take a flower in your hand and

really look at it, it's your world for the moment. I want to give that world to someone else." At the same time, her work set her apart from the male-dominated art world by being uniquely feminine. In the long span of her career—she lived to age 98—O'Keeffe made more than 200 flower paintings, of such varied blooms as roses, daisies, irises, lilacs, orchids, sunflowers and petunias. One of her paintings, of a simple white blossom, sold at auction in 2014 for $44.4 million.

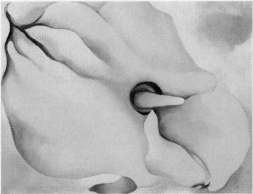

LEISURE

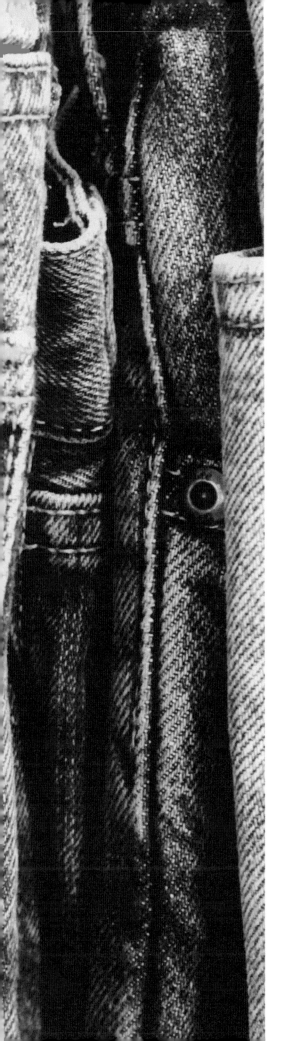

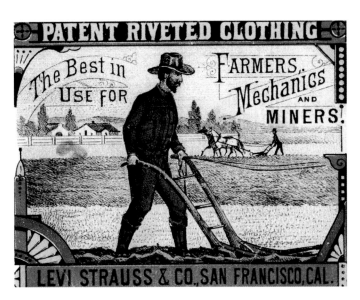

87. Levi's Jeans

LIKE TENS OF THOUSANDS OF AMERICANS, LEVI Strauss got bitten by the gold bug and headed to California in the early 1850s. But instead of panning for nuggets, the Bavarian immigrant settled in San Francisco and opened a branch of his brothers' New York dry-goods store. The population of the City by the Bay had exploded from 812 in 1848 to more than 20,000 in 1850, and young Strauss sold clothes, boots and other items to the new arrivals who streamed into the area seeking quick wealth. One of Strauss's customers was Jacob Davis, a Latvian-born tailor who bought cloth to make tents as well as covers for wagons. The wife of a local laborer asked Davis if he could make durable pants for her husband, and he did so, setting copper rivets at the seams' strain points for reinforcement. He wanted to patent his idea, but he needed help filing the papers and making and promoting the product, so he invited Strauss to be his partner. In May 1873 the two men received U.S. patent No. 139,121 for their "improvement in fastening pocket-openings." They soon started manufacturing pants out of blue denim, calling them "waist overalls" or "overalls." The dungarees, which were perfectly suited to cattlemen, miners and factory employees, became a mainstay of work and casual outdoor life. The U.S. Navy and Coast Guard adopted blue jeans as part of their uniforms in World War II, and by the 1960s, blue jeans had become the unofficial uniform of the counterculture. In the 1980s, jeans morphed once again, into fashion statements—slim, relaxed, acid-washed, low-rise, distressed, boot-cut and on and on—and now some 450 million pairs are sold every year in the U.S.

BLUE SUEDE SHOES

88–91. **American Shoes**

COWBOYS HAVE BEEN AROUND FOR A long time, working on ranches and driving herds. Until the mid-1870s, their footwear consisted of whatever shoes were available, including variations of boots favored by Hessian soldiers and British troops. Then came a German immigrant, cobbler Charles Hyer, of Olathe, Kans., who is credited with being one of the first to make the quintessential cowboy boot. Knowing what a cowhand needed, Hyer devised a new shape, with a scalloped back and front for easy slipping on and yanking off, a pointed toe that smoothly slid into a stirrup and a high, slanted heel to keep the shoe snugly in place. The boot was a success and was quickly adopted by Buffalo Bill Cody, cowboy star Tom Mix and others of the Wild West. Today the footwear is required attire for real and rhinestone cowpokes.

But what's the cowboy-boot equivalent for the urban set? In 1908 Converse started producing work shoes, then branched out with basketball sneakers. By 1917, the company had a catchy name for the athletic footwear: the All Star. America's first mass-produced basketball shoe came in limited choices—high or low canvas and black or white. Four years later, ballplayer Charles Taylor joined Converse's sales force. He worked so hard promoting the shoe and the company that in the 1930s Converse rechristened its sneaker the Chuck Taylor. It became the best-selling basketball sneaker in history. "Chucks," which now double as leisure wear and counter-cultural symbol, earned Taylor induction into the Basketball Hall of Fame.

Film lovers revere a different set of kicks. Although L. Frank Baum gave Dorothy Gale silver slippers in his book *The Wonderful Wizard of Oz*, screenwriter Noel Langley realized that ruby-colored ones would look much better skipping down the Yellow Brick Road in the MGM Technicolor extravaganza. For the shoot, the studio's chief costume designer, Gilbert Adrian, fashioned a number of pairs of sequined silk pumps. In the film, Glinda the Good Witch magically transferred the sparkly shoes onto Dorothy's feet to keep them away from the Wicked Witch of the West. By the time the young Kansan finally realized that to get back home, all she had to do was click them together three times, Dorothy's shoes were transformed into the holy grail of Hollywood memorabilia.

And how about blue suede shoes to reflect youthful rebellion in the face of Eisenhower-era conformity? Carl Perkins, in his autobiography, *Go, Cat, Go!*, wrote that he got the idea for a song about them while performing in Jackson, Tenn., when he heard a boy say to his date, "Don't step on my suedes!" Perkins recalled thinking, "A pretty little thing like that, and all he can think about is his blue suede shoes." That night, Perkins said, he found that his song was "writing itself." Released in 1956, the rambunctious rockabilly tune was the first song to appear on the pop, country and R&B charts and was a hit for Perkins, Elvis Presley and Johnny Rivers.

RUBY SLIPPERS

COWBOY BOOTS

CHUCK TAYLORS

DRAWING THE LINE IN MISSISSIPPI

Berryman 1902

92–93. Teddy Bears and Raggedy Ann

THERE HAS NEVER BEEN A MORE bracing president than Teddy Roosevelt, a Hemingway-esque individual before there was even a Hemingway. But this bear of a man also had an unabashedly boyish quality. A lover of the outdoors, cavalry charges and roughhousing with his kids, he helped the Smithsonian Institution gather specimens of wild animals and insects. During his presidency, he helped establish national parks, forests, bird reserves, game preserves and monuments. Though Roosevelt loved the wild, he also believed that hunting was a noble activity. And his belief in fairness became evident during a visit to Mississippi in 1902, when he and Governor Andrew Longino headed out on a black-bear hunt. The president told his guide, Holt Collier, "I must see a live bear the first day." After hours trudging though the muddy thicket, Roosevelt had no luck finding his prey. Collier then tracked down an old, fat

bear. After the hounds cornered it, he knocked it unconscious and tied it to a tree. The others in the party called out, "Let the president shoot the bear!" But Roosevelt objected, declaring that it was unsportsmanlike and that he would not kill the creature. Hearing of the incident, cartoonist Clifford Berryman sketched an image of Roosevelt refusing to bag a cuddly young cub. The drawing inspired Brooklyn candy-store owner Morris Michtom to place two plush velvet bears with shoe-button eyes in his shop window and call the toys Teddy's bears. Both quickly sold. Not wanting to continue using the chief executive's name without proper permission, Michtom wrote to Roosevelt, who granted it— but added that he didn't think his name would boost sales. How wrong he was. Before long, Michtom and his wife, Rose, were producing Teddy's bears full time.

Another unlikely toy story started with the young daughter of John Barton Gruelle, an Illinois author and illustrator. When the girl, named Marcella, took ill, Gruelle searched his attic for a toy to amuse her and pass the time. He discovered an old doll, but it no longer had a face, so he applied black eyes and a red nose and mouth, then enlisted his mother to fashion a dress. Gruelle entertained Marcella for hours with tales of a kind and trustworthy doll that came to life when humans were not around. After Marcella died at age 13, Gruelle wrote down the adventure stories he had invented for her. He named the toy Raggedy Ann, and in 1915 he received a design patent for her. Soon the Gruelle family began producing yarn-haired Raggedy Ann dolls. In 1918 Gruelle published *Raggedy Ann Stories*, dedicating it "to the millions of children and grown-ups who have loved a Rag Doll." The books were sold along with a doll, and in 1920 a brother, Raggedy Andy, joined in Ann's adventures. Eventually Gruelle created more than 40 Raggedy Ann and Andy books. These floppy rag dolls have been loved by generations of children ever since.

94. Babe Ruth's Bat

THEY DIDN'T CALL GEORGE HERMAN "Babe" Ruth the Sultan of Swat for nothing. For there was never another player like Ruth, who, despite his love of such performance-unenhancing substances as whiskey and cigars, hit a record-setting 714 home runs, notching his bats with a penknife for each new one. As sportswriter Red Smith wrote, "It wasn't that he hit more home runs than anybody else. He hit them better, higher, farther, with more theatrical timing and a more flamboyant flourish." Ruth had legions of fans, but the one who became the most famous was John Sylvester. In 1926 the 11-year-old from Essex Falls, N.J., was deathly ill, and he told his father, "I wish I could see Babe Ruth wallop a homer before I die." His father contacted Ruth's team, the New York Yankees, and Ruth promised, "I'll knock a homer for you."

The team was playing in the World Series against the St. Louis Cardinals, and the Yankees had won only one of the first three games. The day before game four, Ruth told writer Damon Runyon, "The boys ain't hittin', and that's a fact. I know what I'll do. I'll do the hittin' myself." When Ruth went to the plate in St. Louis's Sportsman's Park on October 6, he carried with him a 36-inch, 38-ounce Hillerich & Bradsby Louisville Slugger bat. In the first and third innings, Ruth walloped homers off pitcher Flint Rhem and, in the sixth, another off Art Reinhart, helping the Yankees win the game 10–5. No one had ever hit three homers in a World Series game before, and the trifecta lifted the spirits of little Johnny, whom Ruth visited soon after. It took the lad three years to fully recover, and in 1948, just before Ruth died of cancer, Sylvester visited him to bid farewell to his favorite player. The event was referred to (with several inaccuracies) that year in the film *The Babe Ruth Story*, and Sylvester went on to live until 1990.

95. The Surfboard

THE SURFBOARD IS A PIECE OF SPORTS equipment that has been in development for more than a millennium and a half. Sixth-century Polynesian chiefs rode 25-foot-long boards, and when Capt. James Cook's H.M.S. *Discovery* arrived in Hawaii in 1778, he and his crew watched the locals hit the waves atop the contraptions. Mark Twain even tried surfing during his visit there in 1866, noting how his was a quick ride: "The board struck the shore in three-quarters of a second . . . and I struck the bottom about the same time, with a couple of barrels of water in me." Patience was needed to learn and enjoy the pastime, for as Hawaii native and Olympic gold-medalist swimmer Duke Kahanamoku said, "You know, there are so many waves coming in all the time, you don't have to worry about that. Take your time—the wave will come. Let the other guys go; catch another one." The boards Kahanamoku and others used were large and heavy. Tom Blake changed all that. The Milwaukee native had

met Kahanamoku in Detroit, and "the Duke" encouraged him to seek the warmer climes of California. There he learned to surf. Hoping to make a lighter board, Blake in 1927 transformed an *olo* surfboard—the type used by Hawaiian royalty—by drilling hundreds of holes through the deck and coating it with a thin wood veneer. Friends called his lighter concoction the "cigar box" because of its outline. This hollow plane, which was easier to ride, control and carry, attracted many to the sport and became the first mass-produced surfboard. Innovations arrived as regularly as the next wave. In 1932 the use of balsa wood reduced the board's weight even further. Hawaiian surfers then tapered the tail to help increase maneuverability, and in 1935 Blake added a fixed-tail fin to further increase stability and maneuverability. By then—as the Beach Boys would later croon—all one needed was a board and a dream: "If everybody had an ocean / Across the USA / Then everybody'd be surfin' / Like Californi-a."

96. **Monopoly**

YOU WOULDN'T THINK THAT A GAME about real estate would excite anyone. But since the mid-1930s, Monopoly has brought out the greedy one-percenter in many family members and friends. What better way to pass the time than trying to corner the market on Boardwalk, hoping your opponents get hit with high taxes and tumble into bankruptcy? You might not know that this winner-take-all, last-man-standing game is at odds with its origins. For Monopoly is a version of the Landlord's Game, created by Elizabeth "Lizzie" Magie in 1903. Her board game had four railroads, assorted taxes and lots of places to pay rent. But progressive-minded Magie envisioned it as a teaching tool, writing that "it is a practical demonstration of the present system of land-grabbing with all its usual outcomes and consequences." Magie also had two sets of rules: the monopolist one, in which competitors crush their opponents, and the antimonopolist one, in which all get to share the wealth. Unsurprisingly, the Landlord's Game became popular with liberals and on college campuses. Then, during the Great Depression, Charles Darrow, an unemployed heating engineer, modified Magie's game and sold it to Parker Brothers. Realizing its similarity to the Landlord's Game, Parker Brothers bought the rights to Magie's creation, paying her just $500. Darrow, meanwhile, became Midas-wealthy, like the game's portly, top-hatted character Rich Uncle Pennybags. As the game sold and spread through other lands, the toy maker brought out versions based on foreign capitals, including London and Lagos, and such mythical locales as *Harry Potter*'s Hogwarts School for Witchcraft and Wizardry and SpongeBob SquarePants's home in Bikini Bottom. And, showing the global reach of capitalism, there is even one for communist Beijing.

97. **Facebook**

THERE WAS A TIME WHEN IF SOMEone wanted to hear from you and get a snapshot of your family, they had to wait for a letter in the mail. Not so today. The advent of the Internet and social media has set off a seismic business and cultural shift in which people communicate via snaps and posts and tweets. Facebook led the way. Launched in early 2004 by Harvard classmates Mark Zuckerberg, Eduardo Saverin, Dustin Moskovitz and Chris Hughes, the site mushroomed to a million users by the end of the year. Zuckerberg left college to helm his growing firm, which is now the largest social network in the world, with more than 1 billion users. Half of those on Facebook check in every day. The can't-put-your-phone-down, must-keep-checking site lets users keep up with friends and family, toot their horn, post irreverent memes and videos, "like" others' posts, send messages, and let everyone know of their chang-

98. Mickey Mouse Ears

MICKEY MOUSE IS AN UNLIKELY hero, a chipper rodent with an oversize head and even bigger ears. He may be a little guy, but his success towered over that of his creator, Walt Disney, who once bemoaned, "Fancy being remembered around the world for the invention of a mouse." Although Mickey is one of cinema's most enduring and recognizable characters, he actually started as Oswald the Lucky Rabbit. When Disney's financier bosses appropriated his image, Disney and his colleague Ub Iwerks shortened the rabbit's ears, plumped up his middle and made him a mouse named Mortimer. Disney's wife, Lillian, reportedly didn't like the name, so Disney rechristened him Mickey. The mouse's third screen appearance, in *Steamboat Willie*—the first animation with synchronized music and sound effects—proved to be his star-making role. Other shorts followed, with Mickey often sharing the bill with his girlfriend, Minnie. Disney wisely started to market Mickey merchandise and then launched the Mickey Mouse Club. By the late 1930s, Disney artists were turning out a dozen Mickey shorts a year, with Walt supplying the high-pitched voice until his was ruined by years of smoking. Over time, Mickey retained his plucky personality, but his shape slowly evolved, and in *Fantasia* he even acquired shaky magical powers. A Mickey Mouse hat was first spied in the 1929 short *The Karnival Kid*, in which Mickey tipped his ears like a hat to Minnie. After *The Mickey Mouse Club* appeared on TV in 1955, Mouseketeer Roy "Moose" Williams, who also worked as a Disney animator, created a felt hat with plastic ears. Benay-Albee Novelty Co. was contracted to produce the headwear, which was then sold at the newly opened Disneyland Park. The style took off. Countless sets of mouse ears have since been sold, and while the hat retains its uniquely Mickey shape, it has been continuously updated, with polka-dot patterns, a red bow for Minnie and a golden one to celebrate Disneyland's 50th anniversary. Disney now even offers some with LEDs that sync and glow with the park's evening show.

ing personal and business status. But more than just a friendly way to keep in touch, Facebook is also a news source, a social barometer, an election vote getter, a rallying device for protesters in such places as Egypt, Colombia and Guatemala—and a marketing cash cow. With a current value in excess of $300 billion, Facebook has revolutionized communication and allowed Zuckerberg to join the philanthropy ranks of fellow Harvard dropout Bill Gates, the co-founder of Microsoft.

99. **The Frisbee**

AS A CHILD IN UTAH, WALTER FREDERick Morrison was intrigued by flying saucers. He enjoyed tossing around the lids from popcorn containers and cake pans. After serving in World War II, he molded a sleek-looking disk from plastic and called his creation the Whirlo-Way, after the 1941 Triple Crown–winning racehorse Whirlaway. When reports appeared of a UFO supposedly crashing in Roswell, N.M., Morrison renamed his toy the Flyin-Saucer and then the Pluto Platter. He hawked Pluto Platters on the streets of Los Angeles, and that is where Richard Knerr and Arthur "Spud" Melin, who had just started their Wham-O toy company, saw potential in Morrison's disk. They bought the idea from him and started mass-producing it in 1957. "At first the saucers had trouble catching on," Knerr recalled, "but we were confident they were good, so we sprinkled them in different parts of the country to prime the market." While visiting schools on the East Coast to promote his product, Knerr watched students tossing around pie and cookie tins from the Frisbie Pie Company. As they played, they called out, "Frisbie." Knerr was taken by the name and once again rebranded his product, this time calling it a Frisbee. That was just the beginning. Wham-O went on to sell hundreds of millions of Frisbees. In 1968, competitive Ultimate Frisbee games started in Maplewood, N.J. The sport quickly spread and is now played in 58 countries. In 2014 the International Olympic Committee bestowed official recognition on Ultimate, making it eligible for future Olympic games.

100. The Vince Lombardi Trophy

THERE HAVE BEEN FEW COMpetitors as determined as Vince Lombardi. While studying at Fordham University in the 1930s, he was part of a formidable group of football linemen dubbed the "Seven Blocks of Granite." He went on to play semiprofessional football and then coached his alma mater, the U.S. Military Academy at West Point, as well as the New York Giants. When Lombardi moved over to helm the Green Bay Packers in 1959, the team was in an epic rut. He trained his men like a fanatic. He gave them now-legendary motivational talks, such as: "Winning is not a sometime thing; it's an all-the-time thing. You don't win once in a while; you don't do the right thing once in a while—you do them right all the time. Winning is a habit." His efforts paid off. The Packers became one of the most feared squads in the league, winning five NFL championships and Super Bowls I and II. After Lombardi died in 1970, football commissioner Pete Rozelle named the Super Bowl trophy for him. Created by Tiffany design director Oscar Riedener, the 22-inch-tall silver Vince Lombardi Trophy weighs seven pounds and is topped with a regulation-size football in kicking position. It takes Tiffany four months to make a new one, and after a Super Bowl winner is crowned and the celebrations are over, the statuette is returned to Tiffany for engraving. "When we get back the trophy, it's a cleaning feat extraordinaire," commented Tiffany's Victoria Reynolds on the state of the keepsake after it has been passed around to all the teammates. "We have never gotten a trophy back that does not have champagne on it."

Lucille Ball and *I Love Lucy*

AS A CHILD, LUCILLE Ball wanted to be an actress. She enrolled in a New York drama school, modeled for a while and in 1933 started appearing in small, uncredited roles in Hollywood movies. Bigger parts came, and in 1940 she landed a star turn in the RKO film *Too Many Girls*. The cast included a Cuban bandleader named Desi Arnaz. They married that year but continued their separate careers, Desi making music and Lucy appearing in B comedies. Looking for bigger roles and wanting to work together, the couple in 1951 created *I Love Lucy*, a comic show

that mirrored their married life, with Arnaz as Ricky Ricardo, a serious Cuban bandleader, and Ball as Lucy Ricardo, a housewife yearning for excitement beyond the confines of 1950s-era domesticity. Ball's sharp wit and ditzy slapstick proved a perfect foil to Arnaz's deadpan exasperation. While Lucy's schemes and rebellions inevitably failed, the insanity of her adventures made for classic, rib-tickling TV, including her attempt to join Ricky's band by dressing up as a clown (and displaying her comic chops opposite Harpo Marx) and appearing as an

increasingly tipsy pitchwoman for an elixir called Vitameatavegamin. *I Love Lucy* was the first show with an intercultural couple and the first to feature a pregnant woman. During its six-year run, it was so popular that when it aired, traffic in department stores slowed, as did phone and water usage. The show even bested the Supreme Allied Commander who brought down Adolf Hitler. Dwight D. Eisenhower's presidential inauguration on Jan. 20, 1953, drew 29 million viewers; 44 million tuned in the next day when Lucy's character gave birth to Little Ricky.

TIME

Editor Nancy Gibbs
Creative Director D.W. Pine
Director of Photography Kira Pollack

100 American Originals
The Things That Shaped Our Culture

Editors Kostya Kennedy, Stephen Koepp
Writer Daniel S. Levy
Designer Anne-Michelle Gallero
Photo Editor Liz Ronk
Copy Editor Joseph McCombs
Reporter Elizabeth L. Bland
Editorial Production David Sloan

TIME INC. BOOKS
Publisher Margot Schupf
Associate Publisher Allison Devlin
Vice President, Finance Terri Lombardi
Vice President, Marketing Jeremy Biloon
Executive Director, Marketing Services Carol Pittard
Director, Brand Marketing Jean Kennedy
Finance Director Kevin Harrington
Assistant General Counsel Andrew Goldberg
Assistant Director, Production Susan Chodakiewicz
Senior Manager, Category Marketing Bryan Christian
Brand Manager Katherine Barnet
Associate Prepress Manager Alex Voznesenskiy
Project Manager Hillary Leary

Editorial Director Kostya Kennedy
Creative Director Gary Stewart
Director of Photography Christina Lieberman
Editorial Operations Director Jamie Roth Major
Senior Editor Alyssa Smith
Assistant Art Director Anne-Michelle Gallero
Copy Chief Rina Bander
Assistant Managing Editor Gina Scauzillo
Assistant Editor Courtney Mifsud

Special thanks: Brad Beatson, Nicole Fisher, Erin Hines, Kristina Jutzi, Seniqua Koger, Kate Roncinske, Krystal Venable

CREDITS

FRONT COVER (clockwise from top left) Roland Kemp/Getty Images; Roel Smart/Getty Images; Danita Delimont/Getty Images; mladn61/iStock/Getty Images; Tetra Images/Getty Images (inset); Laura Johansen/Getty Images; Ron Chapple/Getty Images; Brandy Sites/Getty Images **BACK COVER** Henk Meijer/Alamy **TITLE** The New York Times/Redux **CONTENTS 2–3** Bettmann/Getty Images **INTRODUCTION 4** Universal History Archive/UIG via Getty Images **5** (from top) Car Culture/Getty Images; schlol/Getty Images; Silver Screen Collection/Getty Images; Universal History Archive/UIG via Getty images; George Rose/Getty Images; Science & Society Picture Library/Getty Images **ICONIC OBJECTS 6–7** DEA Picture Library/Getty Images **8** Tetra Images/Getty Images **9** Lambert/Getty Images **10** Tetra Images/Getty Images **11** Independent Picture Service/Alamy **12** Photo colorization by Sanna Dullaway for TIME; original image: Library of Congress **13** (clockwise from top left) Jupiterimages/Getty Images; Dcwcreations/iStock/Getty Images; skodonnell/Getty Images; Janine Lamontagne/Getty Images; Brandy Sites/Getty Images; Chiyacat/iStock/Getty Images **14** (from top left) Granger, NYC; GL Archive/Alamy **15** (from left) MPI/Getty Images; John Parrot/Stocktrek Images/Getty Images **16** MPI/Getty Images **17** (from top) Peter Horree/Alamy; Holger Leue/Getty Images **18** Go Nakamura/Redux **19** Bygone Collection/Alamy **MONUMENTS AND BUILDINGS 20** darekm101/Getty Images **21** (from top) Nativestock.com/Marilyn Angel Wynn/Getty Images; Kylie McLaughlin/Getty Images; National Geographic Creative/Alamy; Witold Skrypczak/Getty Images **22** Evan Sklar/Alamy **23** DeA Picture Library/Granger NYC **24** (from top) fallbrook/iStock/Getty Images; Dan Leeth/Alamy **25** Apexphotos/Getty Images **26–27** Jason Moskowitz/Getty Images **27** Irving Browning/The New York Historical Society/Getty Images **28** H. Mark Weidman Photography/Alamy **29** AGF Srl/Alamy **30** Lloyd Sutton/Getty Images **31** (from left) Hulton Archive/Getty Images; ART on FILE/Corbis Documentary/Getty Images **VEHICLES AND EXPLORATION 32** (top left) bitontawan/iStock/Getty Images **32–33** FPG/Getty Images **33** Earl Richardson/Getty Images **34** (from top) Stock montage/Getty Images; Stephen Saks/Getty Images **35** Danita Delimont/Getty Images **36–37** Library of Congress/digital version by Science Faction/Getty Images **37** Tim Gainey/Alamy **38–39** Nik Wheeler/Alamy **40** Apic/NASA/Getty Images **41** (from top) Oxford Science Archive/Print Collector/Getty Images; Granger, NYC **INVENTIONS 42–43** Chris Boswell/Alamy **44** George Ostertag/Alamy **44–45** Chad Ehlers/Alamy **46** Photography by Harry Traeger/Getty Images **47** (from top) Science & Society Picture Library/Getty Images; Ryann Flippo/Alamy; Nicholas Eveleigh/Getty Images; Neil Godwin/Future Publishing via Getty Images **48** Underwood Archives/Getty Images **49** Science & Society Picture Library/Getty Images **50–51** Jim Wilson/The New York Times/Redux **51** (bottom) imagehub88/iStock/Getty Images **52** (from top) Ralph Crane/The LIFE Picture Collection/Getty Images; incamerastock/Alamy **53** (from top) J.B. Spector/Museum of Science and Industry, Chicago/Getty Images; Interfoto/Alamy; Nicholas Eveleigh/Alamy; mgkaya/iStock/Getty Images **54** Bo Zaunders/Corbis Documentary/Getty Images **54–55** Tim Boyle/Newsmakers/Getty Images **56** (from top) Science & Society Picture Library/Getty Images; Sal Veder/AP Photo **57** Hulton Archive/Getty Images **FOOD AND LIVING 58–59** FPG/Hulton Archive/Getty Images **59** Photology1971/iStock/Getty Images **60** phloen/Alamy **61** (from top) Kristoffer Tripplaar/Alamy; WS photography/Getty Images **62** Sean Murray/Getty Images **63** (from top) Davies and Starr/Getty Images (2); Frank Bean/Getty Images **64** Andrew Paterson/Alamy **65** (from top) David Hancock/Alamy; Interfoto/Alamy **66** (from top) ElementalImaging/Getty Images; Zoonar GmbH/Alamy **67** (from top) John Dominis/The LIFE Images Collection/Getty Images; Allison Long/Kansas City Star/MCT via Getty Images **ART AND CULTURE 68** (top left) browndogstudios/Getty Images **68–69** N.A.S./Science Source/Getty Images **70** Courtesy Everett Collection **71** (from top) Sarin Images/Granger, NYC; Apic/Getty Images **72** The Broncho Buster, 1895 (bronze with brown patina), Frederic Remington (1861–1909)/private collection/Bridgeman Images **73** (from top) Sheridan Libraries/Levy/Gado/Getty Images; Michael Ochs Archives/Getty Images; Granamour Weems Collection/Alamy **74** mandj98/iStock/Getty Images **75** JP Jazz Archive/Redferns/Getty Images **76** (from top) Bettmann/Getty Images; Tony Cenicola/The New York Times/Redux **77** GraphicaArtis/Getty Images **78** (from top) Hulton Archive/Getty Images; courtesy Everett Collection **79** Silver Screen Collection/Getty Images **80** (from top) Burt Glinn/Magnum Photos; courtesy W.W. Norton & Company, Inc. **81** Digital image © The Museum of Modern Art/licensed by SCALA/Art Resource, NY/© 2016 The Andy Warhol Foundation for the Visual Arts, Inc./Artists Rights Society (ARS), New York **82** (from left) Bill Hudson/AP Photo; Michelle Williams/Tuscaloosa News/AP Photo **83** (top) John Loengard/The LIFE Picture Collection/Getty Images; (bottom, from left) Terra Foundation for American Art, Chicago/Art Resource, NY/© 2016 Georgia O'Keeffe Museum/Artists Rights Society (ARS), New York; Smithsonian American Art Museum, Washington, DC/Art Resource, NY/© 2016 Georgia O'Keeffe Museum/Artists Rights Society (ARS), New York; image copyright © The Metropolitan Museum of Art. Image source: Art Resource, NY/© 2016 Georgia O'Keeffe Museum/Artists Rights Society (ARS), New York **LEISURE 84–85** Feline Rath/EyeEm/Getty Images **85** Pictorial Press Ltd./Alamy **86** (clockwise from top right) Elnur Amikishiyev/Alamy; imageBROKER/Alamy; dscott/Getty Images; Laura Johansen/Getty Images **87** (from top) Stock montage/Getty Images; Chris Willson/Alamy **88** Sporting News and Rogers Photo Archive via Getty Images **89** Tom Kelley/Getty Images **90** (from top) BeeJay Images/Alamy; photo illustration by Justin Sullivan/Getty Images **91** (from top) Courtesy Everett Collection; David Paul Morris/Bloomberg via Getty Images **92** Michael Paulsen/Houston Chronicle/AP Photo **93** Elsa/Getty Images **94** CBS Photo Archive/Getty Images **END PAGES** (row 1, from left) Encyclopedia Britannica/UIG/Getty Images; Wikimedia Commons; Encyclopedia Britannica/UIG/Getty Images; Wikimedia Commons; (row 2) Wikimedia Commons (5); (row 3) Wikimedia Commons (5); (row 4) Encyclopedia Britannica/UIG/Getty Images; Wikimedia Commons (4); (row 5) Wikimedia Commons (4); Encyclopedia Britannica/UIG/Getty Images; (row 6) Encyclopedia Britannica/UIG/Getty Images (3)

FLAG(S) OF A NATION

As America has expanded, state by state by state, so too has its most powerful symbol

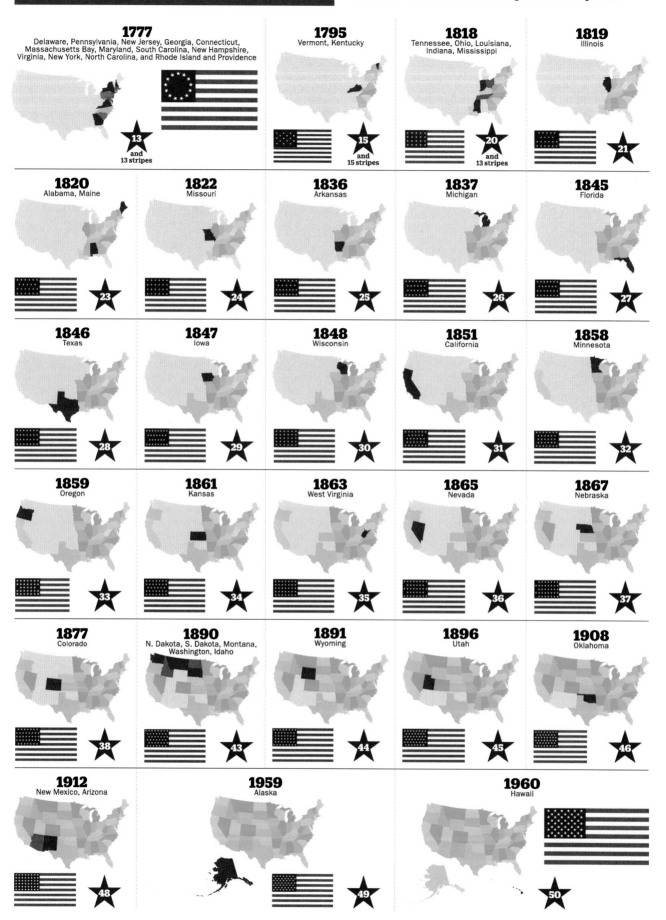

1777
Delaware, Pennsylvania, New Jersey, Georgia, Connecticut, Massachusetts Bay, Maryland, South Carolina, New Hampshire, Virginia, New York, North Carolina, and Rhode Island and Providence
13 and 13 stripes

1795
Vermont, Kentucky
15 and 15 stripes

1818
Tennessee, Ohio, Louisiana, Indiana, Mississippi
20 and 13 stripes

1819
Illinois
21

1820
Alabama, Maine
23

1822
Missouri
24

1836
Arkansas
25

1837
Michigan
26

1845
Florida
27

1846
Texas
28

1847
Iowa
29

1848
Wisconsin
30

1851
California
31

1858
Minnesota
32

1859
Oregon
33

1861
Kansas
34

1863
West Virginia
35

1865
Nevada
36

1867
Nebraska
37

1877
Colorado
38

1890
N. Dakota, S. Dakota, Montana, Washington, Idaho
43

1891
Wyoming
44

1896
Utah
45

1908
Oklahoma
46

1912
New Mexico, Arizona
48

1959
Alaska
49

1960
Hawaii
50

Made in the USA
Middletown, DE
19 September 2019